AFFIRMpress

Eamon Evans is the author of six vaguely funny books, assorted pieces of journalism and an unfinished Masters thesis. His website is www.eamonevans.com.au

Published by Affirm Press in 2015
28 Thistlethwaite Street, South Melbourne, VIC 3205.
www.affirmpress.com.au

Copyright © Eamon Evans, 2015
All rights reserved. No part of this publication may be reproduced
without prior permission of the publisher.

National Library of Australia Cataloguing-in-Publication entry available
for this title at www.nla.gov.au
ISBN: 9781922213778 (paperback)

All design and illustration by Karen van Wieringen
Cover photograph from Caters News Agency
Typeset in 12/19 Garamond Premier Pro by J&M Typesetting
Proudly printed in Australia by Griffin Press

The paper this book is printed on is certified against the Forest Stewardship Council®
Standards. Griffin Press holds FSC chain of custody certification SGS-COC-005088.
FSC promotes environmentally responsible, socially beneficial and economically viable
management of the world's forests.

All reasonable effort has been made to attribute copyright and credit. Any new
information supplied will be included in subsequent editions.

GREAT
AUSTRALIAN
URBAN
LEGENDS

BY EAMON EVANS

To Jenny, Henry, Eliza and my lungs.
You are all very close to my heart.

CONTENTS

INTRODUCTION

What does Kyle Sandilands have in common with *The Bachelor*? And cane toads? And Chiko Rolls?

The answer, I am sad to report, is that none of these things is an urban legend. Just like Schoolies Week and selfie sticks and men with long, hipster beards, these are all actual, real-life things that you can find in Australia. Actual, real-life things that spread misery and social decay. There's no avoiding them, unless you're prepared to skip the country. Which, on balance, might just be a better option than having to sit down and listen to Kyle Sandilands.

But cheer up, folks, and turn those frowns upside-down. For it turns out that a great many of the other bad things that form part of our great southern land are in fact just big, fat myths. Australia is simply bursting with stories that need to be taken with a spoonful of salt. With stories that people *assure* you are true and that you tell others are true in your turn.

Stories like this: 'Hey, did you hear about that BBQ chicken place down the road? (You know, the one near that pizza restaurant that's run by the Mafia? And that mansion where the Masons meet and have orgies?) Well, they just sold someone a chicken from the late 1980s. And, get this, his whole family died.'

So goes a typical urban legend, plus a few more details for extra effect. They're usually something scandalous or silly or sinister or spooky, and they invariably happened to a friend of a friend.

Great Australian Urban Legends gives you myths, misconceptions and bare-faced lies about real people and real places down under. These pages libel Captain Cook and slander Phar Lap; they will piss off AC/DC and David Boon. They ask if Harold Holt really died and if the bunyip ever lived, and which, if any, Australian now gets by as a ghost. They discover underground bunkers, and they find buried treasure. They wonder whether Crown Casino really has its own morgue. This book gives you hearsay and half-truths mixed up with fiction and folktales, then it bakes the result in a big porky pie.

If you think that anything sounds untrue, please remember that that's because *it is*. This book is not called *Great Australian Facts*. Lawyers – kind, sweet, gentle, noble lawyers – I would urge you to please take note of this. And for God's sake, please don't sue.

CAPTAIN COOK

STUBBORN LEGENDS

HISTORY IS WRITTEN BY THE VICTORS, AS SOMEONE ONCE PUT IT – AND WHO KNOWS, THEY MIGHT JUST BE RIGHT.

But let's not forget that history can also be written by people who don't know what they're talking about. People who just half-read, or half-heard, or half-thought something, then half-forgot it and threw in a few prejudices. Our knowledge of the past is like a game of Chinese whispers – one that's played by people who are all slightly deaf and speak with a lisp.

If you don't believe me, keep reading these pages. A lot of the things you 'know' about the past are in fact just a big urban myth.

1770

TERRA AUSTRALIS

It's said that, once upon a time, two cannibals were sitting by a campfire, tucking into a hot bowl of stew. 'God, I hate my sister,' one of them said. 'So just eat the veggies,' his friend replied.

Champagne comedy, I'm sure you'll agree, but Captain Cook probably isn't laughing. The main reason for this is that he's long dead: the man who 'discovered' Australia was killed on a Hawaiian beach in 1779 after a nasty spat with the locals. But the second and perhaps even more important reason is that his body was then eaten by cannibals.

Truly? Well, no. But he *was* cooked. Whatever the reason for Cook's falling out with the locals (and I'm guessing that his attempt to kidnap their king may have had something to do with it), it was a spat that eventually concluded with him getting a big spear right in the back. The locals then carried his body back to their town, and proceeded to honour it in a manner appropriate for the remains of chieftans. This involved a spot of skinning and disembowelling, then putting what remained in a giant oven, so as to more easily tear away the flesh. *Bones*, you see, were sacred to these people. And as a respected elder of his tribe (the British),

Captain Cook's bones were religious relics.

But perhaps the British respect him too much? After all, as at least most of us know, Captain Cook didn't 'discover' Australia. Quite apart from the fact that people have been living here for at least forty thousand years, he wasn't even the first foreigner to come say hello to them. Many historians argue that a Chinese fleet arrived in the early 14th century, and a Dutch ship called the *Duyfken* visited Queensland in 1606. But there's no 'Captain Janszoon's Cottage' in inner-city Melbourne. (Just some house that Cook may or may not have visited, as his parents didn't move there until after he went to sea.)

G⤳CAPTAIN COOK⤳O

Captain Cook probably isn't laughing. The main reason for this is that he's long dead ... But the second reason is that his body was eaten by cannibals.

Cook, then, can only really claim the honour of being the first European to set foot in south-east Australia. And it may even be a stretch to say that. According to tradition, one Isaac Smith was actually the first man to row out from the *Endeavour* and set a pasty white foot on shore.

But even if this story is true (and all Cook ever told us about his eighteen-year-old crewmate was that he was 'a young man' who had 'been of great use'), it doesn't necessarily follow that the 'first European in the south-east' was Smith. Because urban myth has it that, somewhere off the coast of Warrnambool, there lies the remains of a Portuguese ship. You might even be able to find it if you swim a few kilometres out from Armstrong Bay ... and somehow reverse five hundred years' worth of decay.

Sometimes called 'The Mahogany Ship', this mysterious shipwreck was first seen by a trio of sealers whose ship capsized in 1836. As described by George Dunderdale in *The Book of the Bush* (published sixty years later), the sealers

> *succeeded in reaching the shore naked, and then travelled back along the coast to Port Fairy ... On this journey, they found the wreck of a vessel, supposed to be a Spanish one, which has since been covered by the drifting sand. When Captain Mills was afterwards harbour master at Belfast, he took the bearings of it ... Vain search was made for it many years afterwards in the hope that it was a Spanish galleon laden with doubloons.*

And it may have been spotted again in 1848, when a newspaper reported the presence of 'a wreck about two miles on the Belfast side of Warrnambool ... [of a] three hundred-ton vessel ... thrown completely into the [sand] hummocks'.

The idea that this vessel is five hundred years old and *Portuguese* owes a lot to the legend that they were the first Europeans to set foot here (Australia not being far from their colonies in Timor). It's an idea that has a lot going for it. But not, alas, any hard evidence. 🜲

1800s

HAPPY LARRY AND BLIND FREDDY

A good writer always says exactly what they mean, unless they are writing an obituary. When a brand-new corpse has a skeleton in its closet, an obituary becomes an exercise in euphemism; a symphony of nudges and winks. You say that someone was 'good-humoured' if they were a huge alcoholic, and that they 'lived life to the full' if they also did drugs. A 'confirmed bachelor' was a man who lived his life in the closet, and a 'tireless raconteur' was a bore. A criminal was always a 'colourful character', and someone who 'did not suffer fools gladly' was a bit of a prick.

A 'larrikin', however, was a *major* prick. In life, a 'larrikin' is not a bad thing to be, but in death, it tends to mean 'drunken lout'. A drunken lout who was also kind of racist ... though only when he wasn't hassling gay people or cheating on his wife.

Urban legend has it that the first 'larrikin' was 'a youthful prisoner' – one who was hauled up before the Melbourne magistrate some time in or around 1869. His arresting officer, a thickly accented Irishman named

9

Sergeant Dalton, told the magistrate that the prisoner had 'been larking about the streets'. Only, Dalton being a thickly accented Irishman, his first two words sounded like 'being a-larrr-akin'. A journalist who was present used the phrase the next day, and before long it was in common use.

A nice story, but probably not a true one: there's some evidence that the word comes from Worcestershire. According to the *English Dialect Dictionary*, it was used around Bewdley and Droitwich in the early 1800s to describe 'a mischievous or frolicsome youth'.

A happy larrikin, then. Much like Larry. This original 'frolicsome' meaning of 'larrikin' probably also accounts for that other all-Aussie phrase: 'as happy as Larry'.

But urban legend says that this refers to a specific Larry: a boxer from Sydney named Laurence Foley, the son of a respectable schoolmaster, and a boy who gave serious thought to becoming a priest. Larry's career took a different path when he left school at the age of fifteen and joined a violent gang. So talented did he prove at punching people, and then kicking them while they were down, that he eventually abandoned street fighting for prize fighting and started to rake in the cash. Larry retired, enormously rich and successful, for a life of leisure at just thirty-two.

History hasn't recorded whether happy Larry ever saw Blind Freddy. But I think we can be sure that Freddy wouldn't have seen *him*. A baronet who went to Eton, Sir Frederick Pottinger fled England for Australia in the 1850s, after racking up some serious debt on the racecourse, and eventually became a very senior policeman. But this experience didn't stop him from attending a race meet in Wowingragong ... where, in the course of placing

10

a few bets and having a few drinks, he unwittingly mingled with the bushranger Ben Hall. 'Blind Freddy' could have seen that 'Bad' Ben Hall was right there in front of him, but unfortunately Blind Freddy didn't.

So goes the urban myth, anyway: the real story was a little more complicated. But Australians have always enjoyed slandering posh poms. And they enjoy making up urban legends about what those words mean too.

'Posh', for example, supposedly stands for 'Port Out, Starboard Home' and dates back to the days of the British Raj. When wealthy people were sailing from England to India, it's said, they tended to want the bedrooms that would get the most shade. When the ship was travelling east, these rooms were on the left (or 'port') side, and when it travelled home, they were on the 'starboard' (or right). When passenger lines allocated cabins, therefore, they'd write PO and SH on the expensive tickets.

'Blind Freddy' could have seen that 'Bad' Ben Hall was right there in front of him, but unfortunately Blind Freddy didn't.

It's a wonderful theory but for one small problem: passenger lines didn't do that at all.

There's also no record of convicts ever being referred to as 'Prisoners of Mother England', and thus, as some would have it, 'poms'. This theory belongs in the same bin as the legend that 'golf' means 'gentlemen only, ladies forbidden' and a 'cop' is a 'constable on patrol'.

1800s

BURIED TREASURE

'Gold medals aren't really made of gold,' a successful (and rather smug) Olympian once said. 'They're made of sweat, determination, and a hard-to-find alloy called "guts".'

Gold *nuggets*, on the other hand, really *are* made of gold, and it is this fact that makes them so valuable. Australians have been digging for the stuff since 1851, and you don't have to dig too hard to find a few urban legends from our gold rush.

Take the story of Norseman, for example – and, no, I'm not talking about the Western Australian town, I'm talking about the horse which supposedly gave it its name. The story goes that a prospector named Laurie Sinclair was travelling to Esperance one day, when his horse caught a rock in its hoof. Laurie hopped off to lend it a hand, and he discovered that the rock was a nice, shiny yellow. Norseman had uncovered a rich gold reef – a place that's still being mined over a century later, and has produced almost six million ounces to date.

Laurie had the nugget made into a brooch for his wife, and you can still see it, as it happens, because it's often on show at the Western Australia museum. A Cantonese-speaker might describe it as 'ding kam', a phrase that means 'genuine (as opposed to fool's) gold'. Supposedly, it's a term that Chinese miners would use during the Victorian gold rush, when government assayers were inspecting their wares. And it's often said that that's how we got the phrase 'fair dinkum'.

Though on the other hand, 'fair dinkum' may mean 'fair *drinking*'. Miners often liked to gamble at the end of a hard day's digging, and it was considered poor sportsmanship to do so sober. A fair dinkum man was a mildly drunk man: to be clear-headed was to cheat.

Unfortunately, these are probably urban myths too. 'Dinkum' has been part of the English language in Lincolnshire since long before the gold rush, and simply means 'hard work'.

If you don't mind a little hard work yourself, you should try to dig up the land under Brisbane's Albert Bridge. Urban legend is very clear about there being a gold reef hidden somewhere underneath it, which the government refuses to mine or sell. Urban legend is rather less clear as to the *reason* behind this refusal. (Environmental protection of the Brisbane River? The potential for traffic chaos? Some kind of socialist conspiracy?) It's just a *fact* that every assayer who has ever 'been sent in to evaluate the mining opportunities under the bridge has mysteriously vanished', an occurrence that always has the effect of 'stalling plans'.

Plans to dig up Lasseter's Reef have also stalled over the last century or so. But that's largely because it doesn't exist. Australia's most famous hidden treasure was 'discovered' about '250 miles west-south-west' of Alice Springs by a teenager called Harold Lasseter in 1907, when he got lost prospecting for rubies. Alone and on foot, after his horse died from the heat, Lasseter supposedly stumbled across a twelve-kilometre-long reef of gold while half-delirious from hunger and thirst. He would have died. In fact he *should* have died. But he was rescued just in time by an Afghan camel driver. (Or possibly an Aboriginal man. Something like that.)

That, at least, was the story Lasseter told a group of Sydney businessmen in 1940 in an effort to hit them up for some cash. Mission accomplished, he used that money to mount the best-equipped gold-seeking expedition in Australia's history. And he used that expedition to get lost and die.

Lasseter's Reef remains the Holy Grail for Australian treasure hunters. But proper geologists don't think it's fair dinkum. 🐾

ACCIDENTAL LANDMARKS

When it comes to big, bold and iconic buildings, Australia's traditional rivals, Melbourne and Sydney, aren't really rivals at all. Down in Melbourne, there is the MCG (which a cynic might say is just a big sports ground) and that arts centre spirally thing (poor man's Eiffel Tower). And ... well ... that's pretty much it, really. About Federation Square, clearly the less said, the better. (Though I *will* say that whoever designed it should be made to apologise, and then spend a few years in jail.)

Which leaves us with Flinders Street Station. Australia's oldest, biggest and busiest terminus has been called the world's seventeenth most attractive railway station. But if urban myth is to be believed, Melbourne should have had number four.

The story goes that sometime in the 1880s, the powers-that-be decided to spruce up the station, which was then just a smattering of weatherboard sheds. The London firm they hired was certainly qualified for the job, because it was already hard at work on a similar project: designing a magnificent new station for Mumbai. The firm wasn't so much a group of architects as a collective of *artists* – artists with a grand, sweeping vision.

But like many other artists, they weren't all that crash-hot with details. Like the detail of sending the right design to the right city. Some people in Melbourne and Mumbai insist to this day that the latter's Chhatrapati Shivaji Terminus – a grand Gothic masterpiece and UNESCO World Heritage site – was actually intended for Flinders Street. And that Melbourne's quite nice, but not especially striking, station was actually supposed to have been built in Dr Dadabhai Naoroji Road.

The only problem with this story is that the two stations were designed at quite different times. And by quite different architects. But apart from that, it really rings true.

There's no doubt who designed Australia's most iconic building, the world-famous Sydney Opera House. 'To me, it is a great joy to know how much the building is loved,' says the Danish architect responsible, Jørn Utzon, who clearly doesn't realise how much the rest of Australia resents Sydney. Described by UNESCO as 'one of the indisputable masterpieces of human creativity, not only in the 20th century but in the history of humankind', the Opera House has its own semi-mythical creation story when it comes to its original design.

In 1956, the New South Wales government held a competition for the world's best architects to design a grand new building at Bennelong Point. They also invited one of the world's best architects, Eero Saarinen, to help judge all the entries – but, by the time that he finally arrived in Sydney, the judging process was well underway. Quite a few entries had already been culled, and legend says that Jørn Utzon's was one of them. It may have been in a pile of discarded drawings, or it may have been in a bin.

Either way, Saarinen somehow got a hold of the design and gave it two thumbs up. 'Gentlemen, this is the first prize,' he told his fellow judges.

If only that guy had been around when they decided to build Federation Square ...

1909

MYSTERIES OF THE DEEP

If you happened to be thinking about buying a boat, my first question to you would be, 'Why?' My second question would be, 'What the hell do you think you're doing?' and my third, 'Have you told your mum?' Seagoing vessels are dangerous things: just save time and money and try to drown yourself in the bath.

But if you're still determined to go ahead, even after I tell your mum, at least oblige me in this. Don't name your ship the *Waratah*. That name is cursed, I say. Cursed! You may as well call your ship the HMS *Certain Death* or the SS *Fancy a Swim?*

Don't believe me? Here are the facts. Australia's first *Waratah* sank in 1848, killing all thirteen sailors on board. It was joined by two more *Waratahs* in 1887, and yet another one in 1889. By 1895, there were no less than five *Waratahs* mouldering away on our ocean floors.

But sixth-time lucky, as the saying goes. In 1909, a bigtime London shipbuilding company decided to build the biggest and best *Waratah* of all. Over 150 metres long and some 9339 tons heavy, the luxury steamer boasted eight state rooms, one hundred first-class cabins, a spacious music lounge and a fancy saloon. It would be hard to imagine a more stylish way to sail out from the Mother Country and begin a life in the colonies.

That was the theory, anyway. But to put it into practice, migrants needed to actually *reach* the colonies – and this was something that all 211 passengers on board the *Waratah* famously failed to do. The steamer was last seen on the Indian Ocean, by the crew of a passing ship. Its skipper, Captain Phillips, reported that the *Waratah* 'appeared to be perfectly upright and to be in no difficulty' as it disappeared into the mist.

To this day no trace of the *Waratah* has been found, despite over a century of exhaustive searches … but you don't have to search very hard to find an urban myth.

It was never seen again. To this day no trace of the *Waratah* has been found, despite over a century of exhaustive searches. Most likely, it was just capsized by a wave – but you don't have to look very hard to find an urban myth.

The most famous involves a fabled ghost ship. A staple of literature and film (think *Pirates of the Caribbean* if you don't know your Coleridge), the *Flying Dutchman* has been part of nautical folklore for over four centuries. It's a phantom ship with a ghostly crew who, due to some unspecified misdeed in the past, have been condemned to never make land. They must sail the oceans for ever and ever ... And to see the ship is a portent of doom.

Spooky stuff, but don't just take my word for it. Take these words from Captain Phillips:

> *A gale of hurricane force had been lashing the seas when the Waratah passed us. Some hours after I had sent the signal to the liner, I was standing on the bridge when I sighted another ship, a sailing vessel. There was something strangely old-fashioned about her rig. I'm not a superstitious man, but I know my seafaring lore. The rig of the vessel immediately brought to mind the legend of the Flying Dutchman ... the phantom ship held me spellbound. It disappeared in the direction taken by the Waratah, and I had a feeling it was a sign of disaster for the liner.*

Definitely spooky stuff. And even spookier is the fact that one of the *Waratah*'s passengers got off the ship while it was docked in South Africa, after anticipating its demise in a dream. As the *Daily Observer* reported:

One night at sea, [seasoned sea traveller Claude Sawyer]
dreamt of standing on the ship's boat deck staring into the sea.
Suddenly, a knight on a horse rose out of the waves swinging a
medieval sword. A bloodstained sheet was fluttering behind him.
The apparition screamed out 'Waratah! Waratah!' then faded.
Sawyer woke up screaming in his berth. He couldn't sleep after
that but resolved to get off the ship at the next stop.

1915

AWESOME ANZACS, BUMBLING BRITS

'They shall grow not old, as we that are left grow old. Age shall not weary them, nor the years condemn. At the going down of the sun and in the morning, we will remember them.'

So goes the *Ode of Remembrance*, which Australians observe every Anzac Day. By and large, we tend to revere the Anzacs in a way that we've never quite revered the First Fleet. The Gallipoli landing on 25 April 1915 is the real Australia Day for many of us – for it was our nation's baptism of fire.

But are we remembering it correctly? By and large, the answer is no.

For a start, our heroic troops didn't land in the wrong place, as urban legend would have it, thanks to some bumbling Brit. 'It's a common misconception,' says the head of military history at the Australian War Memorial. 'In fact, the Anzacs landed pretty well right in the centre of the originally selected landing zone.' This was a strip of coastline about two kilometres long – and, relatively speaking, it wasn't a bad place to be. What's now called 'Anzac Cove' was well-protected from shellfire and manned by just a handful of Turks.

Myth two is that it was due to further British bumbling that we stayed in Anzac Cove for eight long months, until we finally gave up and sailed off to Europe. While there was no shortage of British incompetence throughout World War I – and the whole Dardanelles Campaign was certainly a bad idea – the Anzacs were actually under orders to march the moment they landed, but instead chose to dig a big trench. 'The first landing was opposed by only about eighty Turks, and the defenders were soon massively outnumbered, but the invaders failed to advance inland as they had been ordered,' says historian Peter Stanley. 'The Australians wanted to blame somebody else for a failure that was basically a failure of Australian command.'

Okay, so what about that scene in *Gallipoli* when some Pommy bastard sends our boys to a certain death so as to create a 'diversion' for British troops? Troops who then spend their time drinking cups of tea, while the Anzacs get mowed down like grass.

Well, for a start, that Pommy bastard was really an Australian bastard. The Battle of the Nek, which the movie depicts, was an entirely Australian operation. And it was designed to create a diversion for *Kiwi* – not British – troops. For history writer Les Carlyon, the scale of the tragedy of The Nek was 'mostly the work of two Australian incompetents, [General Frederic] Hughes and [Colonel John] Antill', while for historian Gary Sheffield, 'Anzac forces were poorly trained and badly disciplined ... Australian troops in time became highly effective, but this was largely the product of experience.'

Without in any way wanting to diminish their sacrifice, it's worth noting that our boys weren't the only ones to die. While more than 8000 Australians lost their lives at Gallipoli, so too did around 34,000 Brits and at least 9000 Frenchmen. Together with soldiers from India and Pakistan and Bangladesh and Nepal. And Newfoundland and Senegal and Russia and Algeria. And let's not forget the roughly 56,000 dead soldiers from Turkey – soldiers who were, after all, defending their country. Urban legend tends to forget that Gallipoli was a human tragedy, not just an Australian one.

More myths? Well, for Gary Sheffield, 'the supposedly egalitarian nature of the Australian Imperial Force has been exaggerated, while larrikinism shaded into racism and criminality.' Also, not all the soldiers looked like Mel Gibson. In fact, the godlike Aussie troops of popular imagination – the tall, tanned and musclebound bushmen who could ride hard, shoot true, shear sheep and make a mean billy tea – mostly came from the suburbs. *And* they mostly wore standard British pith helmets, not those romantic slouch hats.

Okay, just one more disappointment, and then you're allowed to turn the page: they didn't really eat Anzac biscuits. Some such biscuits probably *were* baked by wives and mothers back home, and sent to our brave boys on the front line. But not nearly as many as you might think. As staff at the NZ Army Museum point out, 'the majority of rolled oats based biscuits were in fact sold and consumed at fetes, galas, parades and other public events at home, to raise funds for the war effort. This connection to the troops serving overseas led to them being referred to as "soldier's biscuits".'

They became known as 'Anzac biscuits' some years later.

1926

LORD LAMINGTON AND DAME MELBA

Australia and New Zealand are like siblings. Siblings who don't really get on all that well, yet are at the same time kind of incestuous. If we really *were* an intercontinental family, it would be like one of those dysfunctional ones that you see on *The Jerry Springer Show*, or in a drunken brawl outside the Family Court.

Obviously, none of this is Australia's fault. It's New Zealand's, because they stole the pav. Australia's favourite (well, okay, maybe eighth- or ninth-favourite) desert was famously inspired by a ballerina called Anna Pavlova who toured down under in 1926. It's pretty and light and airy, just like the Russian dancer, a woman who was said to 'soar, as though on wings'.

The one problem with this otherwise rock-solid theory is that Anna also went to New Zealand. And history's first mention of a 'meringue with fruit filling' comes from a book called *Home Cookery for New Zealand* ...

At least we'll always have 'Melba toast'. Legend has it that it was created for our own Dame Nellie Melba by the chef at London's Savoy Hotel. Dame

Nellie was one of those people who are always going on a diet, and then going off it again before her next meal. Urban legend has it that when the opera singer was in one of her diet phases one afternoon at the Savoy – lunchtime having just finished, and dinner being hours away. Feeling a little peckish (it was 3pm, after all), the famously temperamental diva asked the waiter to hurry up and bring her a thin slice of toast. But the chef could only find stale old bread in the kitchen – and it was *so* stale, he had to slice it very, *very* thin. The waiter braced himself for a tantrum. But instead he was smothered in praise.

'Peach Melba' has a similar story, once again set at the Savoy. It's said that Dame Nellie had just finished a four-course dinner, and thus declared herself to be on a diet. This meant that for her fifth course, dessert, she would batten the hatches and just have a small scoop of ice-cream. The chef looked around for something to add to it, found raspberry sauce and peaches, and the first Peach Melba entered the world.

In 1899, however, a koala *exited* the world, and it was all thanks to Lord Lamington, governor of Queensland. Another food-based urban legend tells that His Lordship once inspected a forest which conservationists were wanting him to turn into a national park. Though you could tell that his heart wasn't quite in the proposal by the way he brought along a gun, that site *did* eventually become Queensland's Lamington Park ... and a resting place for one unfortunate koala.

But Lord Lamington is best known today for *another* namesake: a sponge cake garnished with chocolate and coconut. Who exactly created the lamington is one of those questions with a hundred answers. Some say that it was a chef at Queensland's Government House, while others point to a chef at Harlaxton House. Or it could have been someone in Laidley, or someone else somewhere else altogether. All we know for sure is that it's Australian.

So shove that up your clacker, New Zealand.

1970s

FOR THOSE ABOUT TO ROCK

'I'm glad I'm not bisexual,' the English comedian Bernard Manning once reflected. 'I couldn't stand being rejected by men as well as women.'

I don't imagine that the members of AC/DC would ever have had that problem. They may not be the best-looking group of men, but they're rich and they know how to rock.

Also, they're not bisexual. One of the most enduring urban myths about Australia's most enduring rock band is that its name came from a slang term for the sexually versatile. Technically speaking, AC/DC is an acronym meaning 'alternative current/direct current'. But for many of us it means a person who's not all that picky about what's inside pants.

For the sister of Angus and Malcolm Young, however, it was just a strange term that she saw on a vacuum cleaner. When she discovered that it had something to do with electricity and power, she mentioned to her brothers that it might work as a name for their band.

Clearly an ideas woman, Margaret Young also came up with Angus' schoolboy costume. (He'd previously taken to the stage in all sorts of other costumes, including as Spiderman, Superman, Zorro and a gorilla.) Urban legend has always maintained that he started out wearing his uniform on stage because he had to wag school in order to play gigs. But the truth is that he left Sydney's Ashfield Boys High at the age of fifteen, long before the band kicked off.

Like Angus and Malcolm, Jack White also has a sister – but, contrary to myth, it's not his bandmate, Meg. The White Stripes got married, and then divorced, way back when, but are for whatever reason widely thought of as brother and sister.

Natali Germanotta also has a sister – and her stage name is Lady Gaga. A curious myth persists in some places that this singer has a 'micro-penis'. You'll generally find it on the same websites that tell us that Jim Morrison of the Doors is alive and well, while the real Paul McCartney died in the 1960s.

A time of radical change and terrible hairdos, the 1960s were called *The Wonder Years* in the popular 1980s–90s TV show of that name. It starred Fred Savage as Kevin, a slightly awkward teenager who had a habit of pausing during every second conversation, so that a voiceover provided by his future self could say something mildly profound. Kevin's (even more awkward) best friend, Paul, looked like a young Marilyn Manson. And if you believe urban legend, that's because he *was*. If you believe the credits, however, Paul was actually played by an actor called Josh Saviano.

Two other less-than-accurate Marilyn Manson rumours are that he had a rib removed to help him 'auto-fellate', and that he once murdered a basketful of puppies. 'If I'd really gotten my ribs removed, I would have been busy sucking my own dick on *The Wonder Years* instead of chasing Winnie Cooper,' is his only comment on the matter. 'Plus, who really has time to be killing puppies when you can be sucking your own dick?'

Frank Zappa, of course, would never suck his own dick – though some say he's partial to poo. Urban legend has it that the man who named his children Moon Unit, Dweezil and Diva Thin Muffin Pigeen once found himself engaged in a 'gross-out' contest with Captain Beefheart during a concert. When the good Captain did a big dump there on stage, it looked very much like he had won. But then Frank reached for a spoon ...

Or not.

Any more rock'n'roll urban legends? Well, if Stevie Nicks had ever taken a dump on stage, the results may have been worth a quick sniff. The Fleetwood Mac singer was said to have been so addicted to coke back in the day that she sometimes had it blown up her rectum. It is a rumour that she describes as 'absurd': 'Maybe [it] came from the fact that people knew I had such a big hole in my nose ... let's put a belt through my nose, because that's how big the hole is'.

There are, of course, quite a few holes in the human body. And it's apparently possible to fill one of them with fish. Another one of rock's odder legends involves some sexcapades at a Seattle Hotel. Called the Edgewater Inn, it was literally built right on a pier, and allowed its guests to fish right out the window.

In July 1969, some of those guests were the members and entourage of Led Zeppelin – and, being Led Zeppelin, they brought a few groupies. As the band's biographer, Stephen Davis, describes it: 'One girl, a pretty young groupie with red hair, was disrobed and tied to the bed. According to the legend of the shark episode, Led Zeppelin then proceeded to stuff pieces of shark into ...' well, you can probably figure the rest out.

'Word about the escapade spread quickly,' the band's manager wrote later. 'Rumours circulated that the girl had been raped ... that she had been crying hysterically ... that she had pleaded for me to stop ... that she had struggled to escape ... that a shark had been used to penetrate her. None of the stories was true.'

No, these stories weren't true at all. Apparently the boys used a red snapper.

1980s–90s

BILLIONAIRE BOGAN

Not every billionaire is like one of those top-hat wearing, portly capitalists from the olden-day socialist cartoons. They don't all light cigars with $100 bills, and then get some petrol and set fire to the poor. They don't all go big-game hunting and red-Ferrari buying; they don't all bully staff members and cheat on their wives. They don't all begrudge paying a single dollar of tax, and then gamble away millions for fun.

Kerry Packer, on the other hand, did a lot of these things. He was a man with an unlikeable exterior, and on the inside he was a great deal worse.

The former media tycoon did, however, leave us with a whole bunch of legends, some of which may even be true. The most famous are, of course, the gambling anecdotes – like that time Kerry supposedly swaggered into a London casino and put money on four separate roulette tables. He walked out forty seconds later, having lost $15 million.

Or that time over in Las Vegas, when he was hogging a blackjack table all to himself. It's said that some 'loudmouthed Texan' wanted to play alongside him, but was told to 'fuck off' by the (loudmouthed) Kerry because he, Kerry, was playing for 'real money'.

Affronted, the Texan adjusted his Stetson and said that he was a big player too. 'Do you know who I am?'

'No.'

'I happen to be worth $100 million.'

'Toss you for it,' Big Kerry replied – and the Texan quietly resumed his roulette.

To be fair, not all Kerry Packer stories involve him being a giant knob. It's said that on those occasions when he won, he could be a very generous tipper. According to 'an insider' interviewed by biographer Michael Stahl, he once handed over $150,000 to a lucky cocktail waitress because 'he liked the service the girl was providing'. And on another occasion, he pushed US$80,000 worth of chips towards a croupier – only to have the croupier apologise and push it right back. It was casino policy that croupiers couldn't accept tips, she explained. So Kerry called the casino manager and told him to fire her, or he'd immediately take his millions elsewhere.

When the manager obeyed, Kerry handed the croupier the chips. And then told the manager to rehire her immediately.

As threats go, 'taking his business elsewhere' was pretty mild for Kerry, a large man with a steely exterior who kept a large, steely gun in his desk. 'He was a very big man,' recalls his former lawyer Malcolm Turnbull, 'and there was always a slight undertone of menace – sometimes genial, sometimes a sort of mocking menace – but there was always something unsettling about his presence.' Turnbull says that Kerry jokingly threatened to kill him when the pair eventually fell out: 'I didn't think he was completely serious, but I didn't think he was entirely joking either. Look, he could be pretty scary.'

Another employee thought so too, after he happened to ask Kerry, in the course of some small talk, what he thought he would do if someone broke into his office. 'Kerry opened his desk drawer, produced a big handgun and said, "I'd use this", or words to that effect,' a former Channel 9 manager remembered recently.

'He then leaned across the desk and pointed the gun at my head and added: "Which is what I'll do to you if the ratings don't improve," and pulled the trigger.'

SINISTER LEGENDS

'THE ONLY THING WE HAVE TO FEAR IS FEAR ITSELF,' SAID FRANKLIN D ROOSEVELT, PRESIDENT OF THE UNITED STATES, IN ONE OF HISTORY'S LESS INTELLIGENT QUOTES.

If you ever actually got out and *talked* to people, Frank, instead of faffing about with World War II, you would have realised that we have *heaps* of things to fear, for the world is a scary place. Scratch any surface and you'll find something sinister: be it in a park or a street or a school. That sweet-faced old lady might just be a kidney thief. Those people over the road may well poison your kids. Evil is lurking *everywhere* – at least if you listen to some urban legends.

On second thoughts, it's probably better that Frank didn't get out and talk to people. They're a little paranoid, as this section shows.

1960s

BASED ON
A TRUE STORY

Nature is all very wonderful, of course, but it's generally something best seen on TV. If you don't stub your toe when you step outdoors, chances are you'll be stung by a bee. If you don't get sunburnt, it's because you got wet, and if you enjoyed looking at birds, it's because you brought drugs.

Picnics, in particular, are certainly no picnic. They involve flies and ants, and wind and mud. They involve soggy sandwiches and warm, flat beer.

And if one urban myth is to be believed, they can also involve a sinister disappearance. *Picnic at Hanging Rock* is, of course, a 1967 novel that was later made into a Peter Weir film. Set on a hot summer's day in the year 1900, it tells the story of a few girls in a rural boarding school who take a trip to said rock with some teachers – it's a very real and rather spooky-looking place, where many people still picnic today.

Afterwards, however, they tend to go home. Three of these schoolgirls do not. And the novel never once explains why. *Picnic at Hanging Rock* is full of 'breathless silences' and 'strangled cries'. It has flashing lights, mysterious mists and ominous clues like a torn lace collar. To be honest, the whole thing's petrifying: I remember really wanting my mum right after I read it. Which would have been fine, I guess, except that I was about thirty-two at the time.

And what made Joan Lindsay's novel even scarier was the thought that it might all be true. 'Whether this book is Fact or Fiction, my readers must decide for themselves,' wrote Lindsay, in *Picnic*'s preface. 'As the fateful picnic took place in the year 1900, and all the characters who appear in this book are long since dead, it hardly seems to matter.'

But it's certainly mattered to generations of freaked-out Australians who have chosen to take their picnics elsewhere. More morbid (but equally convinced) types have even tried to track down the relevant police records, or uncover clues at Appleyard College, the girls' boarding school.

What makes this task tricky is the fact that the college doesn't exist: *Picnic* is fiction from beginning to end. The idea that there's a grain of truth to the story simply arises from the fact that it's so very well-written and makes reference throughout to various 'newspaper reports'.

But it's *Picnic*'s editor, rather than its writer, who probably deserves the most credit. On the grounds that it's always best to leave readers wondering (and, well, not force them to read complete shit) he persuaded Joan Lindsay to leave out the last chapter of her manuscript – that being the chapter in which all was revealed.

Picnic's 'secret' was finally published in 1987, a few years after Lindsay died. It rather disappointingly revealed that the schoolgirls had been sucked into some kind of supernatural time warp – a time warp that somehow made them into tiny, crab-like creatures that then crawled down a crack in the rock.

See what I mean? Total tosh.

Pardon my language and all that, but 'total tosh' is a phrase that I often find useful when someone insists that so-and-so movie was 'based on a true story'. There was never a *Texas Chainsaw Massacre*, for example, let alone a *Blair Witch Project*. *Fargo* does not depict real-life events that 'took place in Minnesota in 1987', as the Coen brothers say in the credits, and feel free to visit Amityville, New York, any time that you like, because there's no such thing as *The Amityville Horror*.

There's also no need to learn *The Mothman Prophecies*, whatever urban legend would have you believe. And if you're worried about *The Exorcism of Emily Rose*, then to be honest I'm a little worried about you. ✒

1970s

KIDSAFE

Halloween really *was* scary, back in the days when it was 'All Hallows' Eve'. The ancient Celtic tribes truly believed that 31 October was a day when their ancestors came back from the dead. So they dressed up in spooky costumes to scare them off (or at the very least, try to blend).

But for some people today Halloween is *still* very scary, for it represents the eve when their children might die. Even here in Australia, some parents are convinced that, behind white picket fences, there lurk sadists with arsenic-laced lollies just waiting for little Tommy to say 'trick or treat'.

Why on Earth would anyone want to do this? I mean, sure, little kids are annoying, but so are teenagers and adults and the elderly. *People* are annoying, essentially. But the way to deal with that involves TV and alcohol, not baking biscuits that are full of ground-up glass, or making toffee apples with razor blades or pins.

Fortunately, however, little Tommy can munch in peace: the Halloween poisoner only exists in our minds. Trick or treating may well cause car accidents, and help explain rising levels of diabetes and childhood obesity, but it's yet to mask a random act of infanticide by some sicko with a bagful of sweets.

Mind you, the key word here is 'random'. The legend of the Halloween poisoner seems to have begun with an eight-year-old Texan named Timothy O'Bryan, who died from eating a poisoned Pixy Stix back in the 1970s. The American media was consumed by the hunt for his murderer, a hunt which eventually finished at Timothy's front door. It turned out that his murder was not the act of a random nutter; it was the act of a father who had insured his son's life for thousands of dollars and was now trying to cash in. It was a revolting, but far from random, crime. Mr O'Bryan had not been inspired by the Halloween tradition of trick or treating; he had just used it to cover his tracks.

'It was amazing how well-publicised the trial was,' says lawyer Mike Hinton, whose successful prosecution saw the father convicted of murder and sentenced to death by lethal injection. 'There were reporters from London and Germany – all over. Even today it's still talked about ... I think it changed Halloween.'

And while we're on the subject, it's worth noting that you are safe eating toffee apples, and razor blades are a rare sight on waterslides too. If hooligans really *have* been smuggling Blu-Tack and razors onto waterslides – and then somehow stopping halfway down to stick them on, unobserved – then they may as well stop, because it's clearly not working. There are simply no documented cases of any Australian ever getting hurt in this way at all.

Nor have we ever had a razor blade stuck onto monkey bars or some other form of playground equipment. True, there have been one or two cases along these lines in America. But America is a place where about fifteen thousand people get murdered every year, and pretty much everyone else thinks they once saw an alien. It's a fun but deeply crazy country. Be sane yourself, and let your kids out to play. 🐀

1970s

THE DEVIL WITHIN

Some people say that if you play One Direction's first album backwards, you can hear Satanic messages. Personally, I'm more disturbed by what happens when you play it forwards. You can hear One Direction.

Kaboom! Just my little joke. But there are people in the world who really *do* believe that Beelzebub – Belial; the Beast; the Prince of Darkness himself – is lurking in the background of several big rock songs. That somehow, and for whatever reason, the singer is trying to lure you into the hot pits of hell.

Take 'Stairway to Heaven', for example. If you play that backwards, urban legend says, you might just hear the words, 'Here's to my sweet Satan. He will give those with him six-six-six.' Though, I have to say that to my ears, it sounds more like 'klaas jd gi neet asdo' and 'qw zmll iv osd if um zezeze'.

Maybe the Eagles would have had better luck. Some people say that you are only welcome to the Hotel California if you're prepared to abandon Christ. (Well, to be honest, other people say that the song is about insanity. Or drug addiction. Or cannibals. Or cancer. 'Hotel California' is one of those songs that could be about pretty much anything. Although I'm guessing that it's more likely to be about nothing, because the band may well have been high when they wrote it – allegedly, at least.)

The urban legend that says the song is about Satan argues that the Hotel California is actually the Church of Satan, a small organisation of San Francisco 'devil worshippers' that was led by a publicity-hungry wack-job called Anton LaVey. Their 'evidence' for this is that the song says something about killing a 'beast', having a 'feast' and seeing a 'shimmering light' in the distance. And ... um ... well, the album cover looks a bit spooky.

Slightly more plausible is the idea that Hello Kitty is the work of Satan. (Though it's only slightly more plausible for those who are prepared to believe pretty much anything at all.) Hello Kitty, if you're not *au fait*, is a little Japanese cartoon of a cat without a mouth and with a big red bow in her hair. According to Wikipedia, she's a

But there are people in the world who really *do* believe that Beelzebub – Belial; the Beast; the Prince of Darkness himself – is lurking in the background of several big rock songs.

$7-billion-a-year marketing phenomenon that is used to brand everything from school supplies and fashion accessories to high-end consumer products. And according to my niece, she's stupid and her TV show sucks.

Anyway, the story goes that little Kitty was created back in the 1970s by a woman whose little daughter was terminally ill. No doctor could cure the girl's mouth cancer, so her mother turned to Satan instead. The Wicked One agreed to save her life, provided the mother designed a worldwide marketing phenomenon that would appeal to children – and, in some subtle way, market Satan himself.

If so, she succeeded: Kitty's Satanism is very subtle indeed. According to one of those interesting types you meet on the internet, in case you missed it:

> *Hello Kitty was designed with no mouth because the daughter had cancer of the mouth and her pointed ears represent the Devil's horns. The word 'Kitty', meanwhile, means 'Demon' in Chinese. So 'Hello Kitty' really means 'Hello Demon' and anyone who buys Hello Kitty merchandise is welcoming the Devil into their hearts. Satanists all over the world use Hello Kitty as a secret symbol, and many of them actually tattoo the image on their skin. Devil Worshippers refer to Hello Kitty as 'The Daughter of the Devil'.*

In fact, of course, she's the daughter of a Japanese *company*. A small, all-male shoe company came up with the Hello Kitty design, and her name doesn't mean 'Demon' at all.

But God works in mysterious ways, and so too does the Devil. Even though the Dark Lord is so busy appearing in rock songs and helping to sell bags and cosmetics, he has still found time to visit the city of Perth (perhaps it reminds him of hell?). His address there is the big Bell Tower that sits right beside the Swan River. Swans, lest we forget, 'represent traitors, the occult and the DEVIL', while 'the sexual symbolism' of the tower 'is there for all to see'. (The tower, being a tower, is phallic, while the copper 'sails' that swirl around it 'look like vaginal labia'.)

But what clinches the matter (so long as you're slightly deranged) is the fact that the Bell Tower's bells sit 925 inches off the ground, and the tower itself is 3247 inches high. Add 9, 2 and 5 together or 3, 2, 4 and 7 together, and in both cases you come up with 16. This is apparently the number of the Tower card in Tarot, and thus represents the biblical Tower of Babel.

If you have any idea what that means, and why we should care, then please write in and let us all know. 🐀

1979

. . . .

THE LIVING DEAD

When it comes to Australian movies, public opinion is somewhat divided. Some of us think that they're boring, while others simply say that they're dull. Of course, there's nothing actually *wrong* with making a film about some person who's miserable, and then gets steadily more miserable while not doing much. What's wrong is expecting us to watch it.

There are, of course, some glorious exceptions to this rule: *Gallipoli*, *The Castle*, *Crocodile Dundee*. (I also quite like *Strictly Ballroom*, but I'd rather you kept that to yourself.) And then there's *Mad Max*. Up there, at the top of the class. Once described as 'the granddaddy of all dystopian action extravaganzas', *Mad Max* depicts a post-apocalyptic Australia that's been torn apart by an energy crisis and is now dominated by big bikie gangs. Clad in leather, and chock-full of crazy, they zoom up and down the desolate desert highways, raping, looting and pillaging – and performing all manner of cut-price stunts.

And when I say 'cut-price', I mean *really* cut-price. Filmmaker George Miller shot the movie in twelve weeks with just $350,000, and that meant no money for fancy stuntmen or special computers producing 'special effects'. *Mad Max* features real bikes going really fast. And real bikies bleeding real blood.

But, contrary to rumour, it doesn't feature a real death. 'There's an urban myth that a stuntman was killed. That was me,' says the alive-and-well Dale Bensch, a member of Melbourne motorcycle club the Vigilanties, whom Miller recruited to come do their thing. 'The scariest thing [in Dale's famous "stunt" scene] was dropping the bike on that bridge. They took the speedo and tach off because they didn't want to damage it more than they had to ... but I hung on to the bike too long and it flipped me over with it; that's why it looked bad. But it's a famous scene, so it worked out all right!'

If you believe urban legend, however, and are a tiny bit sadistic, there are still plenty of other movies you can hire in order to see someone 'really' die. A stuntman 'really' died during the *Ben-Hur* chariot race, for example (though history is strangely silent when it comes to his name). And you can actually *see* the moment that actor Brandon Lee was accidentally shot on set (even though the director used an earlier take in the final scene of *The Crow*).

An even more popular belief that's no more (and no less) untrue is that – along with singing and dancing and a loveable dog – *The Wizard of Oz* features a real-life suicide. Google Image the scene and you'll find that you can see a sort of shadowy figure in the distant forest, as Dorothy & Co make their way up the Yellow Brick Road. And from a certain angle (if you're of a certain mindset) that figure could be hanging from a noose.

Or then again, it might be a peacock. That's what the filmmakers themselves always said – and given there were dozens of such birds wandering around the stage set of *Oz*, and no actual record of any crewmembers dying, I'm going to go out on a bit of a limb here and say, 'Who knows? They might be right.'

But that's certainly not a peacock in that scene in *Three Men and a Baby*, where Ted Danson walks past a window in his flat. That's a little boy, or something. Just there, hiding behind the curtain. But there's no little boy in the script, my friends, so what in tarnation is going on? Should *Three Men and a Baby* be retitled *Four Humans and a Ghost*?

This legend is simply *everywhere* on the internet, despite the movie being almost thirty years old. Received opinion is that it's the ghost of a kid who used to live in the flat, and whose death sent his mother insane. *Intelligent* opinion, however, is that the 'ghost' is actually not a ghost, but a cardboard cut-out of the Ted Danson character. His character, you see, is an actor – an actor who lends his image to a dog food commercial (with associated 'standees') in a part of the film that was later cut. (Sounds good, but I'm not buying it. The dog food, I mean. The explanation makes sense.)

Anyway, if there really *was* such a thing as a ghost in a film, we would have found it in a recent James Bond. Did you know that the actress who played the Bond girl in *Goldfinger* actually died after being covered in gold paint? We 'breathe' through our skin, do you see?

Or do you not see? That's probably for the best. That Bond girl, Shirley Eaton, is still alive and well.

1980

THOU SHALT KILL

The Seventh-day Adventist Church was founded in 1831, when a mathematically inclined Baptist preacher from New York state worked out that the second coming of our Saviour was just twelve years away. 'My principles,' William Miller wrote, 'are in brief that Jesus Christ will come again to this earth, cleanse, purify, and take possession of the same, with all the saints, sometime between March 21, 1843, and March 21, 1844.' It was imperative, he declared, that God's children get themselves ready, and the best way to do that was to buy his book.

If you imagine that Miller lost a few followers on 22 March 1844, then you clearly haven't met too many Americans. Sure, their 'fondest hopes and expectations were blasted' and they 'wept, and wept, till the day dawned', but it wasn't long before the Adventists all realised that their leader's only mistake was that he mucked up the maths. The church has gone from strength to strength over the past 150 years, and it now has eighteen million members all over the world. Generally speaking, they believe that Christ is due to come any day now, and that George W Bush was a pretty good president.

One thing they *don't* believe in, however, is the divine importance of human sacrifice. (That, or Obamacare.) This is a fact that should really go without saying, but back in the 1980s, Australians said something else. Lindy Chamberlain, you see, was a Seventh-day Adventist, and her husband was an official church minister.

If you're young and those names don't ring any bells, I give you the words 'dingo' and 'baby'. When the Chamberlains took their three children on a camping trip to Uluru in 1980, they famously returned to Mount Isa with two. Nine-week-old Azaria vanished from her tent, while her parents were somewhere nearby. The couple insisted that she must have been taken – and presumably eaten – by a dingo, and a coroner eventually agreed.

That coroner, however, was the fourth to turn his mind to the case. And he didn't agree until the year 2012. The Chamberlain case has been the subject of four inquests and a lengthy Royal Commission – not to mention a murder trial which Lindy famously lost. A slightly odd and very emotionally detached woman, who never quite knew how to handle the media, Chamberlain spent three years in prison before new evidence emerged, which quickly led to her acquittal in the Supreme Court.

She received $1.3 million compensation for wrongful imprisonment, but what about compensation for all the urban myths? 'Azaria', you see, means 'sacrifice in the wild' (even though it actually means 'gift of God'). The child's 'murder' was part of a ritual to atone for Lindy's many sins – a ritual accompanied by 'the faint strains of religious music' and carried 'under the shadow of the great Uluru'. (Like all good sacrificial altars, it's a big, broody monolith in the middle of nowhere, that turns blood red in the hot desert sun.)

Want more? Well, Australians were convinced that Lindy had liked to dress Azaria in black, and once built a little white coffin for her in her garage. As noted at the time in some anonymous fan mail, Lindy was a 'hard-faced, cruel-eyed monster and a witch' who had shed not a tear at the funeral. In her Bible she had circled that bit from the Old Testament, where a woman called Jael lures some guy into her tent, helps him fall asleep and then smashes his skull.

'The Chamberlain murder trial polarised the Australian community,' wrote one commentator of Australia's OJ Simpson moment – a TV ratings hit rivalled only by *Neighbours* and our big win in the America's Cup. 'The miscarriage of justice, the relentless media scrutiny and the mediaeval-style public condemnation of Lindy Chamberlain all exposed the prejudices of mainstream Australia.

'When the Chamberlains were convicted, and Lindy got life imprisonment – recoiling, mouth gasping, like someone who had been shot – there was thunderous applause throughout Australia.'

1990s

I SEE DEAD PEOPLE

Unless a person happens to be seriously depressed, or seated between two accountants at a particularly long dinner party, they will never, in the course of life's journey, find themselves yearning for an immediate death. Resting in peace is something that we all tend to put off for as long as we possibly can.

Sometimes, however, it just strikes out of nowhere. The grim reaper gets tired of waiting and starts to swipe away with his scythe. Just like the other night at Revolver (a super-hip bar and nightclub on super-shit Chapel Street, Melbourne). As I'm sure you would have heard, this guy who was wearing sunglasses sat down on the couch for a bit of a kip. When the cleaners came along on Monday morning, he was still sitting on a couch wearing sunglasses. And had been dead for almost three days.

Such stories are not uncommon (though they are, of course, also not true). Everybody's got an anecdote about a corpse in the workplace, just like the one of 'George Turklebaum'. George was a 51-year-old New York publisher, working in an open-plan office with twenty-three other employees. He suffered a fatal heart attack at his desk, and his body was left unnoticed for five whole days. 'George was always the first guy in each morning and the last to leave at night,' his [mythical] boss told a [mythical] newspaper.

'So no one found it unusual that he was in the same position all that time and didn't say anything. He was always absorbed in his work and kept very much to himself.'

But not all dead bodies like to keep to themselves. Legend says that you'd unearth a crypt if you ever got a huge saw and started hacking away at the pylons that hold up the Sydney Harbour Bridge. It's said that when the bridge was being built, back in the 1930s, two or three foreign labourers were accidentally trapped inside it, but nobody noticed until much too late.

A rather less well-hidden corpse, if another urban myth is to be believed, belonged to the Dead Granny of the Nullarbor Plain. Much like Bernie in *Weekend at Bernie's*, and whoever it was in one of those *National Lampoon* vacations, this granny is said to have carked it right in the middle of a road trip ... and in the middle of the desert as well. Her family was days away from any kind of township, let alone a hospital or morgue. So what were they supposed to do once she started to smell? What else but tie her to the roof?

Walt Disney may also be a little smelly by now, unless you happen to like liquid nitrogen. But that's just what happens when you have your body cryogenically frozen, so he has no one to blame but himself. One of the 20th century's more persistent urban legends is that Disney did not actually die from lung cancer, but is just resting, like King Arthur and his knights of the round table, ready to make a return. His body is supposedly in storage underneath Disneyland, in preparation for the day someone can come up with a cure.

Walt's resurrection will be all the more remarkable when you consider the fact that he was actually cremated in California's Forest Lawn cemetery. And that the first recorded instance of cryonic preservation occurred long after his death. No one knows who started the rumour or why, but if you're reading this, then congratulations. It's a good one, big tip of the hat.

The rumour that *Hitler* didn't die, on the other hand, was less entertaining. And we now know that it was started by Stalin. When the Soviet army stormed into Berlin in 1945, they found Adolf's corpse burned and buried near his bunker, along with that of his mistress Eva Braun. The couple had wisely chosen to kill themselves rather than face the righteous wrath of the world.

You'll still find books that say Hitler and Braun lived it up in fascist Argentina, until he passed away in 1962.

But, for whatever mysterious, Cold War-related reason, the Soviet leader initially decided to deny that he had proof that Hitler was dead, and always refused to let any Westerner examine the body. The myth grew that the German mass-murdering moustache-wearer had in fact managed to make his escape. You'll still find books that say he and Braun lived it up in fascist Argentina, until he passed away in 1962. 🦇

1990s

MELBOURNE'S UNOFFICIAL MORGUE

Federation Square lies at the heart of Melbourne, and you could say that the MCG represents its soul. The Yarra is the city's lifeblood, and the universities serve as its brain.

Crown Casino, on the other hand, is a kind of wart or fatty pustule. Not as ugly perhaps (its architecture's actually quite nice), but hardly an asset to the health of the city – unless you happen to like watching pensioners go broke. Gambling destroys as many lives as drug use, and to my mind it's not nearly as fun.

Perhaps God was trying to tell us this when the casino opened in a blaze of glory (and corruption allegations) way back in the 1990s. Designed along feng shui principles (Asian high rollers being highly superstitious), the shiny new casino had an elaborate opening ceremony that culminated in a flock of white doves being symbolically released into the starry night sky.

Doves are supposed to represent hope, peace and purity. But these ones represented bad planning. The story goes that they were all burnt to a crisp by those big fire-belching thingies that Crown Casino has lined up outside.

'Is the roasted-dove tale true?' the writer Meg Mundell once wondered. 'Crown insists it's an urban myth, but won't confirm that no doves were harmed.'

'No birds were burned at the opening,' a spokeswoman told Mundell. So the birds were fine? '"No, they weren't fine ... But that was a long time ago. It's not to go in your story." She then clammed up: no further comment.'

So who knows? But if the doves really *did* die, Crown might at least have had a good place to put them. Another allegation that's annoyed casino administrators over the years is that they also administrate their own private morgue. It's said to be buried deep underneath the building and to accommodate all the punters who pass away from heart attacks, or lose all their money and reach for a knife. 'What's more,' says the *Herald Sun*, 'particular bathroom cubicles are said to have such a high suicide rate that they're actually engineered to rotate for quick body disposal. Presumably this is so the next visitor to the bathroom isn't deterred from further gambling by discovering two Crown employees wheeling a corpse down the hallway.'

We should point out that many people deny that Crown has an underground morgue. Though this is because they believe it has an underground *tunnel to* a morgue – the official one, at Royal Melbourne Hospital. Others say there's some kind of chute down there, which runs right into the river. So if urban legend is right, the next time you see a corpse floating down the Yarra, that person probably had a bad set of cards. ❧

2000

RAMBO GRANNY

Grandmothers are a source of unconditional love, a wellspring of cuddles and treats. They buy you presents, they bake you cakes and they let you watch whatever you want on TV.

But what they *don't* do, as a general rule, is hunt down rapists and shoot off their testicles. A Melbourne octogenarian called Ava Estelle proved the exception to this rule in the year 2000, after two men bashed and raped her beloved granddaughter. 'When I saw the look on my Debbie's face that night in the hospital, I decided I was going to go out and get those bastards myself, 'cause I figured the police would go easy on them,' the 81-year-old former librarian told the *Weekly World News*. 'And I wasn't scared of them, either – because I've got me a gun and I've been shootin' it all my life.'

Armed with a 9mm pistol, and a profound knowledge of Melbourne's mean streets, 'Granbo' looked high and low for two men who matched Debbie's description – and eventually tracked them down. Convicted robber Davis Furth, thirty-three, and his former cellmate, Stanley Thomas, twenty-nine, were hiding out in a seedy hotel room. But there was no hiding from Granbo's wrath: 'I knew it was them the minute I saw 'em, but I shot a picture of 'em anyway and took it back to Debbie and she said sure as hell, it was them. So I went back to that hotel and found their room and knocked on the door – and the minute the big one, Furth, opened the door, I shot 'em ... right square between the legs, right where it would really hurt 'em most, you know. Then I went down to the police station and turned myself in.'

As the story goes, she put the gun on the sergeant's desk and said, 'Those bastards will never rape anybody again, by God.'

Apparently the men, though seriously injured, were mostly relieved to have survived the wrath of Granbo.

Detective Evan Delp told the *Weekly World News*: 'What she did was wrong, but can you really throw an 81-year-old woman in prison, especially when all three million people in the city want to nominate her for sainthood?'

Armed with a 9mm pistol, and a profound knowledge of Melbourne's mean streets, 'Granbo' looked high and low for two men who matched Debbie's description.

If this story sounds unbelievable, there's a pretty good reason why. The *Weekly World News* is a satirical newspaper. It's the sort of news source that will tell you that Elvis is not only alive and well, but he's also been having a sordid affair with the Loch Ness Monster. Its stories look and read like they might be true, so long as you're not very bright.

But back to crime-fighting: it's time to talk about 'the choking Doberman'. You know, that dog who belonged to that friend of your friend. Let's call her Mary. No, scrap that: Sue.

Anyway, Sue, as you know, went out to dinner with a couple of friends one night (or perhaps she caught a film or a play). The dinner (or film or play) was all perfectly pleasant, but when she returned to her Sydney (or Melbourne or Adelaide) apartment a few hours later, her evening took a turn for the worse. She opened the door, heard a strange, spluttering sound, and realised that her dog was somehow choking to death.

Panicking, Sue rushed the dog to the nearest animal hospital. The vet there examined him a bit, looked up 'choking' on Google, and then told her that he'd need to perform an emergency tracheotomy – a complicated procedure that would take most of the night.

'Go home and get some rest,' he kindly suggested. 'I'll call you when we have some news.'

So go home Sue did, but rest she did not, as the vet called her almost straight away. 'Get out!' he urged, rather breathlessly, without even a 'Hello, how are you?' 'GET OUT NOW and call the police!'

So get out Sue did, and into her apartment went the police. They found a notorious rapist passed out on the floor of her bathroom, blood gushing from his mangled right hand.

The vet had discovered why the dog was choking. Three fingers were lodged in his throat. ⟡

2001

RAT ATTACK

The world is a dangerous place, but not necessarily in the ways you might think. Sharks, for example, barely hurt a soul. We're talking maybe five deaths a year. And that's five deaths a year, worldwide.

Plane crashes? Nope, not really. The odds of you being killed next time you take a flight are roughly one in fourteen million – statistically, you're a lot more likely to die from a nasty fall off your couch. And it's worth noting that the last Australian to die from a spider bite did so during the 1970s. Sure, a redback might not make an ideal pet for a child, but it's far from one of nature's great predators.

Falling coconuts, on the other hand, really *do* kill people (so long as they're standing under the tree at the time). Vending machines somehow cause at least ten deaths a year (in what you might call a modern example of natural selection), and tens of thousands of Americans are no longer with us because they fell out of their beds. You and I may have nothing to fear but fear itself, but stupid people also need to be careful that they don't end up blowing themselves up with deodorant cans or drunkenly cutting off their own heads to impress their friends. (These have both actually happened.)

One final warning, dear reader, and then I'm afraid you're on your own. Please, please exercise caution the next time you hammer a nail into your dick. According to a widely circulated 'news' report, a man from Fremantle just wasn't careful enough one hot summer's day in 2001.

It's said that 32-year-old Bruce Coltraine was hard at work restoring some furniture when his mind began to wander south, to his pants. So he put down his hammer and started to masturbate – until inspiration struck and he reached for a nail. A bit of self-piercing could be a turn-on, Bruce reasoned, so he placed said nail on his foreskin, grabbed the hammer and gave it a whack.

Unfortunately, the nail slipped. And pierced the penis itself. It was *not* a bit of a turn-on. Screeching, weeping and dizzy with shock, Bruce reached for a cold bottle of Coca-Cola and poured it all over his injury, in the hope of easing the pain. Then he passed out, and who can blame him?

You'd think that this was as bad as things got for young Bruce, but unfortunately you would be wrong. When he woke up several hours later – pale, frail and covered in blood – he was no longer the man that he had been. Drawn to the sugary Coke (and, to be fair, many of us are), a bunch of rats had started gnawing away at his willy, and then gone on to swallow his scrotum.

Bruce died on his way to hospital. Which was quite a feat, given he never actually lived. 🐀

2010s

KILLERS, RAPISTS AND KIDNEY THIEVES

It's said that evil lurks within all of us – that civilisation is just a thin and fragile veneer, beneath which lies a savage beast. We're only nice because society makes us be nice. We only care because we are told to.

This is possible, I suppose, in the sense that anything is possible – the Earth might be flat; the Richmond Tigers might win a flag; Kim Kardashian might become an interesting person. But personally I rather doubt it. Look at the face of a baby and you'll see innocence, not evil. (Though you may smell evil if you go near their nappy.)

Anyway, the subject of babies and evil brings us to our next urban myth (and you can't say that that's not a smooth segue). There's no thin veneer of civilisation surrounding the crybaby serial killer: he's just pure psycho from head to toe. Hard at work in towns and cities all over the country (and often in two or three cities at the exact same time), this murderer's modus operandi involves an old-fashioned cassette player and a cassette tape of a crying baby. He will put it in a pram and press *play*, then walk to a woman's house and knock on the door. 'My baby is sick,' he will yell frantically. 'You really must let me in.'

And if she does, you can guess what comes next.

Grim. And also untrue. The man is a worldwide myth. 'If the public was in any danger or if there was any truth to it, we would let the public know,' said a Louisiana Police Department spokeswoman, when a rumour of that nature was mentioned. 'We have no reason to believe it is true.' So relax next time you hear a crying baby.

But maybe *don't* relax if someone gives you a $5 note. Urban myth insists that there's a sweet, pleasant-looking man in some suburb in Northern Sydney who's in the habit of knocking on a single woman's car window, just as she's getting ready to drive away from a shop. 'I just saw you drop this,' he will say, oh so pleasantly, flashing a smile full of shiny white teeth. And in his tanned hand, he'll have a $5 note.

If you believe urban myth, don't unlock your car door. It will unlock the door to abduction and rape. But if you believe the *police*, I'd say that you're probably safe: versions of this story are told all over the world, but you don't often hear it in court.

Of course, not all sexual horror stories have to involve rape – a consenting partner can have a hard time too. The late 1980s and early 1990s were filled with stories about a man and a woman who met in a pub, flirted a bit and had a fine old time. After a date or two, or an hour or two (or a couple of minutes if they were feeling a bit frisky), the pair made their way to the woman's house and got it on without using a condom.

But the next day, sad to say, she woke up alone – or, rather, all alone except for a little white envelope. She opened it, expecting to find a phone number or perhaps some words of praise for that thing she did with the cucumber. But instead she found just five scary words: 'Welcome to the AIDS club.'

Harrowing, yes. True, no.

Anyway, there might be worse ways to wake up. For example, waking up in a bathtub full of ice, all covered in bandages and with a *horrible*, searing pain in your tum. The next time you go on a holiday – or, indeed, any sort of trip that involves travelling alone – please be careful to not have a drink with a stranger and then pass out because they just slipped you a drug.

The world, you see, is simply *full* of criminals who steal and sell kidneys on the organ transplant black market. It really is a heartless crime. But then again you're kidney-less, so let's not throw stones. ☙

2010s

THE OTHER ROAD TOLL

Cars are responsible for a lot of what's wrong with the world, from pollution and rising obesity, to Jeremy Clarkson and the cast of *Top Gear*. But if urban myth is to be believed, things could actually be even worse. Beneath their bland steel exterior, cars can conceal all sorts of maniacs (and, no, I'm not still talking about Jeremy Clarkson).

Car myth one involves a shopping centre in Western Sydney. It's said that a woman once parked there and went in to buy something, and then found her car window smashed when she returned. Within seconds, a man wandered up to her, saying that *his* car had actually been stolen. Could she please give him a lift to the police station? They should both report the crimes asap.

'Okay,' she replied, 'but I just want to check in with the security guard first.'

'No,' said the man, there was no time to lose; they needed to get in the car right *now*. Something about his insistence made her turn around and run. When, ten minutes later, she returned with a security guard, they found a knife and a gun hidden underneath her passenger seat – and, of course, no trace of the man.

Frightening, yes. Factual, no. The story has also been set in shopping centres in a dozen other parts of Sydney, and in quite a few other cities as well.

Car myth two is also set in a car park, but this one stars a sweet-faced little old lady. A sweet-faced little old lady with a bad case of arthritis ... who was in fact a somewhat-less-than-sweet man. A young woman offered the hobbling arthritis sufferer a lift, but noticed her thick, hairy legs just before opening the door, and promptly sped away.

Every now and then, however, we really *do* give strangers a lift, and it's thanks to this fact that I can give you myth three. Every book that's ever been written about urban legends will eventually mention 'the vanishing hitchhiker', so who am I to break with tradition (or, indeed, do original research)?

Minus the minor variations (it's a legend told all over the globe), the story involves someone driving all alone, somewhere in the countryside late at night, who sees a figure waving a thumb by the side of the road. Nobly, the driver stops and offers the person a lift, and he or she clambers into the back. This strangely pale passenger says next to nothing as they speed through the dark down the road, and then after a while they say nothing at all. The driver glances into the rear-vison mirror and discovers the reason for this: their passenger has vanished into the thin night air.

Days later, the driver makes a second discovery. A person exactly matching that passenger's description has been dead for a great many years.

Spooky stuff, as I'm sure you'll agree, but wait till I give you myth four. Our final car legend involves two teenagers who get it on in 'Lover's Lane' or 'Passion Peak' or some such faux-romantic location. Picture them pawing away in the back of a car, sultry music helping the mood. Then imagine a newsreader interrupting the radio broadcast with some rather ominous news. A convicted murderer has just escaped from a nearby jail – a convicted murderer who has a hook for a hand. Anyone who sees a person matching that description 'should immediately leave the area and report the matter to the police'.

For the teenage girl, this is something of a mood killer. She rolls over and reaches for her bra. The boy, on the other hand, is no quitter, and he does his best to try and convince her to stay. He tries the shoulder rub, the ear nibble, the 'Oh please, Babe, I'm so horny', but it is all to no avail. She wants to drive home and she wants to drive quickly – and so, eventually, he starts the car.

When they arrive at the girl's house, relations are still frosty, and she gets out with nary a word. Within seconds, however, she has plenty of words; the girl starts to scream uncontrollably, face white and eyes wide with shock. The boy gets out and looks at the door handle. Dangling from it is a bloody steel hook.

SILLY LEGENDS

'PEOPLE WILL BELIEVE A BIG LIE SOONER THAN A LITTLE ONE,' SAID DR WALTER C LANGER, THE DISTINGUISHED AMERICAN PSYCHOANALYST WHO WAS FAMOUSLY BORN WITHOUT TOES.

And you can see his point. If a politician tells us that they're going to lower marginal tax rates, most of us won't really believe them (in my case, I just won't understand). But if they announce that we're fighting a 'War on Terror', we're more than prepared to believe it – why would you lie about *that*? When someone said that we could eat as much fat as we liked, so long as we went easy on carbs, half of us went out, bought bacon and started frying a few extra eggs. Silly urban legends have all sorts of sources – but most of them simply start out with someone's big lie. A lie so ludicrous, so out there, so *patently ridiculous* that we all figure it *has* to be true.

Incidentally, that was a lie about Dr Langer's toes.
As far as I know, he had ten.

1800s

ALL CREATURES GREAT AND SMALL

If half of the things foreigners thought about our wildlife were true, it'd be a bloody miracle that you and I are alive. Australia, it's said, is simply awash with deadly animals – from snakes and spiders, and stingrays and sharks, to predatory sea snails and poisonous caterpillars. To walk outdoors is to dance with death. To go in the ocean is to go to your grave.

Or not. According to most estimates, our animals only account for about five deaths a year. That's not much in a country of twenty-three million people. You may as well worry about getting struck by a lightning bolt, or coming down with a bad case of the plague.

But what about all the deadly creatures that we can't see? No, I'm not talking about that tiny tick that may be lodged in your intestine, or a scorpion so poisonous it could kill your whole family. I'm talking about five or six deadly creatures which are so very, very inconspicuous that you will *never* see them.

European colonists have a long and glorious tradition of 'spotting' unfamiliar animals in the unfamiliar bush, then doing some casual pinching

74

and twisting of Indigenous stories to serve as explanations. Bunyips, for example. Possibly inspired by the fossils of the diprotodon (a sort of ancient wombat that was the size of a hippo), this creature lurks in our riverbeds by day. And it emerges at night in order to feast on our young.

Bunyips in the know, however, stay away from the riverbeds by the Hawkesbury, for there lurks the lethal moolywonk. A few 19th-century settlers claimed to have spotted a large, lizard-like, sort of Loch Ness monsterish creature in the area, and there's certainly something very like that in local rock art. But unfortunately, nothing very like it has ever been caught.

Perhaps this is because we're all too busy looking for muldjewangks? Said by some

But what about all the deadly creatures that we can't see? ... I'm talking about five or six deadly creatures which are so very, very inconspicuous that you will *never* see them.

people to be a race of mermen, and by others to be a sort of serpent, muldjewangks can be seen in the Murray River in South Australia – so long as someone with paper and a pencil is prepared to sit down and draw you a picture.

If all these swamp creatures are putting you off swimming, I'm afraid that you're no safer on land. For, as you know, Australia's gum trees all conceal little predators that like to leap down and feast on the contents of your skull. The most prominent of these is the drop bear: a large, carnivorous koala with huge claws and big, sharp teeth.

But it also pays to be aware of the yara-ma-yha-who. 'Four feet tall and sporting bright red skin', this creature has some interesting table manners, according to a writer named Shell Harris.

> When a yara-ma-yha-who spots its prey, it will jump down on top of them and suck most of its blood. It uses octopus-like suckers on the ends if its fingers and toes to hold on while it feeds. After the victim is sufficiently weakened, but still alive, from blood loss, the yara-ma-yha-who will swallow them whole. After falling asleep, the yara-ma-yha-who will then regurgitate its victim. Upon waking, they will swallow the victim again. The process of eat-and-regurgitate will continue over and over again until the victim, who is usually alive throughout the entire process, becomes a new yara-ma-yha-who.

Good times. Though I myself would prefer to become a yowie. These creatures are, after all, at least *vaguely* human, despite being twelve feet tall and covered in hair. Sightings of Australia's version of Bigfoot date back to at least 1795, and supposedly number in the thousands. 'Who has not

76

heard, from the earliest settlement of the colony, the blacks speaking of some unearthly animal or inhuman creature … namely the Yahoo-Devil Devil, or hairy man of the wood?' wrote a journalist in 1876.

There are also quite a few hairy cats in the wood, so I'd suggest that this hairy man watch his step. Big cat sightings are a standard feature of suburban newspapers: editors practically set aside a page for them. Australia's big cats include the 'Tantanoola tiger', the 'Lithgow panther', the 'Cowra cougar' and the 'beast of Buderim'. There's a 'puma' in the Grampians, a 'tiger' in Jamberoo, and, at a conservative estimate, about 6.2 billion 'panthers' prowling around the outskirts of Melbourne and Sydney.

Some people say that these cats are the descendants of an animal that escaped from the circus. Or related to an American army mascot that was here during the war. But sceptics have an even more sensational theory, which, if you're sitting down and can strap yourself in, I'll take a deep breath and share with you now.

They're just a few random big, feral cats … 🐾

1908

· · · · · · · · · · · ·

LOST IN TRANSLATION

Canberra is one of those places that are really great to leave – not so much a big country town as a sort of post-apocalyptic suburban wasteland. You could walk Canberra's bland, empty streets for well over a month, and never once find a full pub or bar. About the only place you'll ever see a crowd is in the airport on a Friday night. Whether they be Labor or Liberal, National or Green, our nation's policymakers all have at least one policy in common, and that is 'whenever you can, get the fuck out of Canberra'.

Fortunately, Melbourne and Sydney are both pretty close. Appropriately enough for a place that feels like someone put a film set in the middle of a desert, Canberra is quite literally the middle of nowhere. A dryish, largely empty floodplain, it was chosen as the site for Australia's capital in 1908 because it was more or less halfway between our two largest cities – and because, hey, we all make mistakes.

That floodplain's name, 'Kambera', most likely comes from the now-extinct Ngunnawal language, and the urban myth is that it used to mean 'meeting place'. Kambera was a place where warring tribes could gather – and where they still do to this day.

But the far more appealing reality, according to at least one Ngunnawal elder, is that the word actually refers to the fact that Canberra is a flat plain nestled between two mountains. Our nation's leaders, this is to say, are all gathering in a town called 'Breasts'.

For many people, I imagine, this prospect would be a little more appealing than gathering up someone's bum. But according to another urban myth, 'up the bum' is exactly where people from Melbourne go when they get together to celebrate Moomba.

The story goes that when the Melbourne City Council decided to mark the Labour Day weekend with an annual festival, way back in 1951, they asked a local Aboriginal elder if he could come up with a catchy name. 'How about "Moomba"?' so-and-so suggested. 'It means "let's all get together and have fun".'

But maybe he was the one having fun? '"Moom" means "arse", it's as simple as that,' says the Indigenous historian Gary Foley.

There's a similar story about Goodna, a 'shit' suburb in the south of Brisbane. The story goes that when white settlers arrived in the area, and ordered its inhabitants to make themselves scarce, they also asked one of the local Aboriginal people what exactly the area was called. 'Goona' he or she answered. A word which, according to legend, actually just meants 'shit'.

The 'kangaroo' story is also a load of shit, if we believe the linguist John Haviland. But I myself prefer not to; it's just too good a tale. Urban legend has it that when Captain Cook and crew stopped on the banks of what is now Cooktown to carry out repairs on the *Endeavour*, they also conducted a little more research into the large, bouncy creatures they'd seen at Botany Bay. 'What is it called?' Cook reportedly asked one of the local Guugu Yimidhirr people, when one such creature went bounding past. 'Gangaroo,' he helpfully replied.

Or perhaps he wasn't actually being that helpful? To this day, many people insist that the word 'kangaroo' is actually a phrase. A phrase that means something along the lines of 'I'm sorry, but I don't understand'. ☻

1966

ALIENS CAME TO CLAYTON

I've always wondered why aliens bother coming to Earth, when they always just get up and leave again after a couple of hours. Scientists say that our closest potentially habitable planet, 'Kapteyn b', is still trillions of kilometres away. It seems a long way to go just so you can fly over a few outer suburbs, or abduct a truck driver from Chesapeake, Ohio.

But hey, apparently it happens. And what's more, it's happened right here. Australia's most famous alien encounter occurred on 6 April 1966 in the outer Melbourne suburb of Clayton. No less than two hundred students and teachers say they saw a saucer-shaped, silvery-grey object float over the sports ground at Westhall High School for about twenty minutes before slowly descending into a nearby paddock and then, very abruptly, flying off.

Roughly twice the size of 'two family cars', the flying saucer 'had a sort of purple hue to it', according to one witness, and an underside that 'seemed to thicken at times'.

'I couldn't tell you what it was,' reports another witness, who was riding a horse in the paddock at the time. 'I saw the thing come across the horizon and drop down behind the pine trees,' Shaun Marshall told *The Age* a few decades later. 'And [then I] saw it leave again. [It] went up and off very, very rapidly.'

'I went over and there was a circle in the clearing. It looked like it had been cooked or boiled, not burnt as I remember. A heap of kids from Westall Primary and High School came charging through to see what had happened – "look at this, look at that, we saw it as well", that sort of thing. It was a bit of a talking point for a couple of days.

'The way this thing moved, there is no way it could have been a weather balloon or a light aircraft.'

Okay ... well, what about a helicopter, then? 'No way,' says Shaun. 'No noise, wrong shape, and it didn't move like it ... It didn't just sort of cruise and then slightly descend at an angle. It just stopped, dropped, and then went straight up.'

Golly. So what the hell was it, then? Two hundred people can't all be lying (unless every single one of them happens to be a real estate agent – or a mechanic who just serviced your car). For years, our best clue was the fact that the paddock was 'quickly cordoned off' just minutes after the UFO finally flew away, and 'personnel in camouflage gear took charge'. Meanwhile, the school headmaster 'gathered everyone together for an assembly ... flanked by men in suits or uniforms, and he made it very clear to everyone that there was no such thing as flying saucers'. The students were instructed to not talk to the newspapers. And indeed the media barely mentioned the incident at all.

So, some kind of secret military thingamajig? Some action movie-style experiment that all went a bit wrong? That's always seemed like the most plausible explanation, and these days it's pretty clearly the right one. National Archive documents that were unearthed in 2014 have revealed that the Australian government ran something called the 'HIBAL program' during the 1960s, after it allowed Britain to conduct nuclear tests at Maralinga.

HIBAL involved sending high-altitude balloons all over Australia to measure whether or not radiation levels had significantly increased – something that the government understandably wanted to keep quiet, given that voters don't like it when politicians give them leukaemia. The balloons were silvery grey, about the size of two cars, and carried heavy machines underneath. They could well have looked like an 'upside-down cup and saucer' to the untrained eye.

Moreover, one particular archive indicates that a test balloon launched from Mildura was blown off course, and towards the suburb of Clayton, on one especially blustery April day. ☠

1970s

THE MAN WITH NO FACE

There are a lot of crazy rumours going around about Mel Gibson. Like that he's been accused of domestic violence, and homophobia, and sexism and racism. Like that he has said: 'the Jews are responsible for all the wars in the world'. Like that he's had both his stepmother and a girlfriend file restraining orders against him, and has implied his ex-wife is going to hell. Like that he belongs to an extremist Catholic sect which believes that men and women are 'not equal'. And that he has a father who thinks the Holocaust is 'mostly fiction'.

As it happens, all these rumours are true. Mel's what you might call an interesting fellow. But we should make one thing very clear for the record: he's a man with his own face.

One of the odder urban legends about 'our' Mel is that, back when he was an anonymous teenager, he was waylaid in the street by five thugs. But instead of just handing over all his money like a sensible person and begging for mercy with a tear in his eye, the future Mad Max got mad. He threw a punch at the first thug, aimed a kick at the second ... and then fell to the ground as they proceeded to beat him to within an inch or two of his life. According to someone on the internet: 'They mashed his face with their boots, and kicked and beat his body brutally with clubs, leaving him for dead.'

Mel hadn't lost his life – no, far worse than that: he had lost his looks. 'Each eye socket was smashed ... his nose was literally hanging from his face, all his teeth were gone, and his jaw was almost completely torn from his skull.' But God works in mysterious ways. It's said that, after Mel spent the next five years working at a circus freak show, and about five thousand hours praying in church, his priest was able to secure the services of Australia's best plastic surgeon – and I think that we can all agree that he did his work well. Fame and fortune followed for Mel, his just reward for putting faith in the Lord.

This deeply silly story was presumably inspired by *The Man without a Face*, a movie (with a completely different plotline) which Gibson starred in and directed himself. But the actor's 'big break' may have also had something to do with it. Mel largely got the role of Mad Max, that battle-scarred, mildly psychopathic 'road warrior', because he arrived at his audition with a 'busted-up face'. A week or so earlier, as the actor once recalled in a *Playboy* interview, he'd got into a drunken brawl at a party (as one does) and 'woken up in the bloody hospital with head stitches, a busted nose, my jaw off the hook, peeing blood'. It was the look that the casting agent was going for: Mel's just reward for being a little bit nuts.

Of course, quite a few Hollywood stars have woken up in a hospital over the years, if 0.00001 per cent of plastic surgery rumours have any truth.

There's simply not enough room in this book to tell you who the 'experts' believe has had a little nip here, a little tuck there, and a truckload of silicone shoved into their chest.

Let's just say that Hollywood's wig-wearers are rumoured to include John Travolta. And Ben Affleck and Matthew McConaughey. And Al Pacino and Edward Norton.

Cher, meanwhile, is supposed to have had a few ribs removed in order to achieve an ultra-slim waist. Though the same rumour seems to have dogged pretty much anyone who happens to have an ultra-slim waist – a category that has included Elizabeth Taylor, Jane Fonda, Raquel Welch, Tori Spelling, Kate Moss, Janet Jackson, Britney Spears and Pamela Anderson.

If only Hollywood could realise that you don't need plastic surgery to make you happy. You can just eat factory-farmed chicken. Rumour has it that plenty of young boys out there are starting to develop a rack just like Pamela Anderson's, simply by eating a few hormones and chemicals. Call it a cut-price alternative to surgery. Or, better yet, call in a doctor. ☻

1978

. . . .

THE VALENTICH DISAPPEARANCE

It's sometimes joked that a rabbi, a minister and a priest were all aboard the *Titanic* the day that everything went tits-up. As people started piling onto the lifeboats, the rabbi heroically stepped aside, yelling out, 'Women and children first!' The minister, rather less heroically, replied, 'Fuck the children!' And the priest said, 'Do we have time?'

Fortunately, I would never make a joke like that: Catholic priests are no laughing matter. And nor, for all that, are shipwrecks. Australian history is littered with boats that vanished beneath the waves, and now rot on our ocean floor. And the ones that sank in the 'Bass Strait Triangle' have given rise to urban legends as well.

That long, narrow channel that divides Tasmania from the mainland, the Bass Strait Triangle actually looks more like a trapezoid. But just like its Bermuda namesake, the strait has seen hundreds of ships get wrecked – and at least two dozen just disappear. The most famous vanishing act was that performed by the HMS *Sappho*, a British warship with over one hundred crew. It set sail from Sydney in 1858, and never arrived at a port.

All very sad, of course, but hardly spooky, since Bass Strait is a sailor's nightmare. Its strong currents from the Indian Ocean clash with strong currents from the southern Pacific. Huge rocks are here, there and everywhere, along with sudden waves and treacherous reefs.

So not a good place to take a boat. But you'd think that a *plane* would be perfectly okay. The 'mystery' of the Bass Strait Triangle – at least as far as urban legend is concerned – began with the disappearance of a military aircraft while it was searching for a lost ship in the 1920s. Two more planes disappeared in the 1930s, and an unspecified number of bombers went down during training throughout World War II.

In 1972, yet another light plane disappeared. But it was the 'Valentich Disappearance'

It was the 'Valentich Disappearance' six years later that put the matter beyond any doubt: some kind of alien was clearly involved.

six years later that put the matter beyond any doubt: some kind of alien was clearly involved.

On a still October evening in 1978 – a still October evening during a week in which Australia experienced 'dozens of UFO sightings and reports of unexplained lights' – a young pilot named Frederick Valentich set off from Melbourne across the Bass Strait a few minutes before 7pm. At 7.06pm he radioed the Melbourne Flight Service to report that an aircraft was following him. This is a transcript of the conversation that followed:

Frederick Valentich [FV]: *Is there any known traffic below five thousand [feet]?*

Melbourne Flight Service [MFS]: *No known traffic.*

FV: *I am – [there] seems [to] be a large aircraft below five thousand.*

MFS: *What type of aircraft is it?*

FV: *I cannot affirm. It is [sic] four bright, it seems to me like landing lights ... The aircraft has just passed over me at least a thousand feet above.*

MFS: *Roger, and it, it is a large aircraft? Confirm.*

FV: *Er, unknown due to the speed it's travelling. Is there any Air Force aircraft in the vicinity?*

MFS: *No known aircraft in the vicinity.*

FV: *It's approaching right now from due east towards me ...* [Silence for 2 seconds.] *It seems to me that he's playing*

*some sort of game. He's flying over me two, three times, at a
time at speeds I could not identify.*

MFS: *Roger. What is your actual level?*

FV: *My level is four and a half thousand. Four five zero zero.*

MFS: *And confirm you cannot identify the aircraft.*

FV: *Affirmative.*

MFS: *Roger. Stand by.*

FV: *It's not an aircraft. It is—*[Silence for 2 seconds.]

MFS: *Can you describe the, er, aircraft?*

FV: *As it's flying past, it's a long shape.* [Silence for 3 seconds.]
[Cannot] identify more than [that it has such speed]. [Silence
for 3 seconds.] *[It is] before me right now, Melbourne.*

MFS: *And how large would the, er, object be?*

FV: *It seems like it's stationary. What I'm doing right now is
orbiting, and the thing is just orbiting on top of me also. It's
got a green light and sort of metallic. [Like] it's all shiny
[on] the outside.* [Silence for 5 seconds.] *It's just vanished
… Would you know what kind of aircraft I've got? Is it
military aircraft?*

MFS: *Confirm the, er, aircraft just vanished.*

FV: *Say again.*

MFS: *Is the aircraft still with you?*

FV: *[It's, ah, nor-]* [Silence for 2 seconds.] *[Now]*
approaching from the southwest ... The engine is, is rough
idling. I've got it set at twenty three twenty four, and the
thing is—coughing.

MFS: *Roger. What are your intentions?*

FV: *My intentions are, ah, to go to King Island. Ah,*
Melbourne, that strange aircraft is hovering on top of me
again. [Silence for 2 seconds.] *It is hovering, and it's not an*
aircraft. [Silence for 17 seconds, open microphone, with
audible, unidentified staccato noise. End of transcript.].

The world never heard from Frederick Valentich again. And no trace was
ever found of his plane. ☻

1980s

THE DARK LORD OF WANG

Located 'just two and a half hours north of Melbourne' and boasting 'daily rail services to Sydney', the 'historic town' of Wangaratta 'provides the ideal base to tour Victoria's gourmet region'. Along with 'a labyrinth of activities such as performing arts, cultural and musical festivals', it offers up 'an endless array of fine food' and 'superb wine', plus 'an atmosphere to suit any mood'.

That's if you believe the Wangaratta tourist bureau, anyway. If you believe Nick Cave, it's 'a fucking horrible town'.

'It was a difficult place to grow up,' says the 'grand lord of gothic lushness', and his life there was 'fucking misery'.

Ah well, each to their own. I dare say that most small country towns have their share of broody, disaffected artistic types whose habit of poncing about in black skivvies quoting Nietzsche means that they never quite find a way to fit in. Tortured singer-composer-poet-actor-author-screenwriters are actually everywhere in Australian society. We just don't tend to realise because they're disguised as waiters, or behind the counter at KFC.

Nick Cave, however, we *have* noticed. Fantastically successful for almost four decades, this one-time junkie uses an 'eclectic hybrid of blues, gospel, rock and post-punk' to explore his 'obsessions with religion, death, love, America and violence'. (Or something like that, anyway.) He's a man who can write a song about smashing a woman's head in, and then sing it on *Top of the Pops*.

But does he actually write songs in blood? One of the more enduring urban myths about the 'Prince of Darkness' is that he jots his tunes down with a blood-filled syringe. And, strangely enough, there's a small sniff of truth to it: it's said that the Gothic One once needed to write a letter while he was taking a trip on the Tube, but couldn't quite get his hands on a pen ...

My favourite Nick Cave story, however, concerns his co-singer in that famous 'murder ballad', 'Where the Wild Roses Grow' – the rather-less-than-gothic Kylie Minogue. An urban legend says that the Dark Lord's London flat wasn't actually the den of iniquity his fans might have felt entitled to expect during the late 1980s. There were no open coffins. There were no ancient cobwebs. There was no old junkie's corpse in the cupboard. The flat was, instead, rather light, clean and airy ... and filled with 'posters and paraphernalia' of Ms Kylie Minogue.

Cave is happy to admit that 'Where the Wild Roses Grow' was written with Minogue in mind. 'This song, even though it's a murder ballad, is dealing with a kind of obsession I had with her – on a professional level, but an obsession – which is about her beauty and her innocence, in a way.'

Maybe it would have been easier to use a pick-up line? Another Australian rocker reportedly did just that with the Singing Budgie – and they ended up an item for years. The 'archetypal rock showman', Michael Hutchence was not just a singer who, in the words of rock historian Ian McFarlane, 'exuded an overtly sexual, macho cool with his flowing locks, and lithe and exuberant stage movements'. He was also a bit of a smoothie.

The story goes that Minogue met Hutchence for the first time at an INXS concert, when she was taken backstage by her then-boyfriend, Jason Donovan. The rocker took one long look at her, ignoring Donovan entirely, and said, 'I don't know whether to take you out for lunch or have sex with you.'

They ended up doing both. 👾

1980s

THE DEAD CAT

Cat people are smarter than dog people, according to an American psychologist. Being a dog person, I would like to take issue with Professor Denise Guastello, whose publications include 'Dynamics of attitudes and genetic processes' and 'Birth category effects on the Gordon Personal Profile variables'. But I'm not entirely sure I'd be able to understand what she's talking about.

Anyway, we all know that Malcolm Turnbull's a dog person. The former Rhodes Scholar and all-round smartie-pants even has a 'dog blog' on his personal website that contains musings 'from' his Maltese silky cross. He even wrote a touching obituary for Mellie, JoJo's three-legged sister, when she passed away in 2012.

'Why do we love dogs so much?' Malcolm wrote. 'Is it because they are loyal and loving? Is it because they love us for what we are, without judgement? How can it be that in a world of so much human tragedy, so much momentous and terrible change, we shed tears over the death of a little white dog? Is it because, as Byron said, our dogs have all the virtues of man, without his vices?'

All very sweet, I'm sure you'll agree. Especially for a man who occasionally goes hunting ...

But it's worth noting that Malcolm's writings on the subject of animals may not quite stop there. According to an age-old urban legend, he also wrote a letter to a cat back in 1981 while he was in the midst of a tumultuous break-up. The cat, Nessie, belonged to his newly-ex-girlfriend, Fiona Watson. And let's just say that it seems she wasn't the one who was heartbroken.

According to the always-reliable internet, the letter read as follows:

> *Dear Nessie,*
>
> *Tell your miss that I love her very much, tell her that when I came to see her on Sunday and she wasn't there I cuddled you up and it broke my heart that it wasn't her.*
>
> *Tell her I know a lot about her current boyfriends will tell her not to see me, they will stroke her back and tell her to forget me.*
>
> *But, Nessie, we know she never will and you tell her, my little cat, how much we were in love.*
>
> *all my love*
>
> *Malcolm*

But the myth part is also about what comes next. The slightly ludicrous story begins with Fiona returning home a few days after finding this letter to discover that her cat is dead. She apparently believed that it had been strangled, and her (unnamed) neighbours had reportedly 'seen Malcolm around the house at the relevant time'.

'No cat has died at my hands,' is all that Malcolm will say about the matter.

Other than that he was 'very upset' about the rumour, and imagines that the cat just 'got run over by a car'.

Former media mogul (and convicted felon) Conrad Black had a different take, however. According to Black's autobiography, Malcolm 'allegedly punctuated an altercation with a friend by sneaking into her home late at night and putting her kitten into the freezer, transforming a frisky pet into a well-preserved corpse'.

I myself have no opinion on the matter, other than that I don't like getting sued. Perhaps we should all just agree that Malcolm seems like a dog person. ☠

1980s

ANOTHER DEAD CAT

People who say that 'crime doesn't pay' don't seem to understand economics. Crime clearly pays *heaps*, you idiots – just pick up a newspaper and read. We are living in a world that's filled with billionaire drug barons, and more or less financed by white-collar crime. And don't forget all those 'dole bludgers' and 'queue jumpers' that you read about in the tabloids. According to *A Current Affair*, these people are *everywhere*. Throw a brick and you'll probably hit one now.

What *is* true, however, is that not *all* crime pays. There is obviously money to be made by stealing an iPad, or selling some teenager a bagful of smack. But I, for one, just can't see the profit in purloining a handbag that is filled with dead cat.

A popular urban legend (which is sometimes set overseas) involves a Perth woman of indeterminate age and race who headed out to the Hay Street Mall shops. She parked her car, started walking along the footpath – and abruptly stopped when she saw a dead cat. Being a lover of said species (and, let's face it, a little bit odd), the lady decided that she couldn't let this poor creature just be put in a bin by some anonymous council employee. Like all of God's creations, it deserved a decent burial – and it looked like the job was hers.

First, however, she had some shopping to do. So the woman opened a bag, filled it with cat, and went off on her merry way.

Good times were had, good purchases were made, and then suddenly it all went bad. A dastardly criminal appeared on the street, snatched one of her bags and made himself scarce.

You can probably guess which bag. 💀

I, for one, just can't see the profit in purloining a handbag that is filled with dead cat.

1997

EMBARRASSING DEATHS

'We've all got our self-destructive bad habits,' says David Lee Roth of Van Halen. 'The trick is to find the four or five you personally like the best and just do those all the time.'

Good advice, David, provided you choose with care. It would appear that Michael Hutchence did not. The archetypal rock'n'roll frontman (right down to the drug problems, insecurity and depression), he committed suicide while 'under the influence' and distraught about a custody case involving his daughter.

The INXS singer's body was discovered on the morning of 22 November 1997 in an upmarket Sydney hotel. Police reported that 'he was in a kneeling position facing the door. He had used his snake skin belt to tie a knot on the automatic door closure at the top of the door, and had strained his head forward into the loop so hard that the buckle had broken.'

And by the afternoon, the myth-making had begun. Despite the findings of both an autopsy and a coronial inquest, and the parade of witnesses citing his shaky state of mind, many people will still confidently tell you that Hutchence didn't commit suicide, but accidentally died from a sex act. 'Autoerotic asphyxiation' essentially involves using a rope or a belt to cut off the flow of oxygen to your brain, and then getting busy with a nice, quiet wank. According to Wikipedia, it does wonders for your orgasms, but I think I'll just take their word for it.

Anyway, this interesting hobby doesn't only raise eyebrows; it's been known to cause death. And on the rare occasions that this happens, other people have been known to laugh. It's not, all things considered, the *most* dignified way to depart this planet – but according to urban myth, there are worse.

Mama Cass, for example, may not have been the sveltest member of The Mamas and the Papas, but she was a woman who knew how to chew. It may be 'common knowledge' that she choked to death on a ham sandwich, but it's also completely untrue. The heavily overweight singer simply died from a heart attack: no food was ever found in her windpipe.

It's also true that no food was found in Tennessee Williams' windpipe. But what about a bottle cap? According to a widely read report at the time, the playwright may have choked to death trying to open a bottle of nasal spray with his teeth. It's a story that tends to stick in the mind, but drugs are now thought to have been the cause.

Either way, eating a bottle cap could well prove healthier than a life spent on the Atkins diet. Urban legend has it that the creator of this controversial high-fat, low-carb 'nutritional approach' actually ended his days weighing 117 kilograms – and, of course, died from a heart attack.

King Adolf Frederick would have enjoyed the Atkins diet. Much like that romantic hero Attila the Hun (a man who drank himself to death at his wedding), this Swedish monarch liked to let himself go. It's said that, after eating his customary courses of lobster, kippers, caviar, sauerkraut, herring and lobster at a banquet one day, he insisted on fourteen servings of his favourite dessert. The last one broke the camel's back. Or, rather, it broke his stomach.

Arius, a third-century theologian, also had tummy troubles. While scholars still remember him as a

It may be 'common knowledge' that she choked to death on a ham sandwich, but it's also completely untrue.

'proto-monotheist' whose 'opposition to the Homoousian Trinitarian Christology made him a primary topic of the First Council of Nicea', I myself tend to think of him as that guy from history who accidentally shat out his bowels.

According to one of Arius' political opponents: 'A faintness came over him, and together with the evacuations his bowels protruded, followed by a copious haemorrhage, and the descent of the smaller intestines. Moreover portions of his spleen and liver were brought off in the effusion of blood, so that he almost immediately died.'

Nasty. But not as bad as dick rot. Herod the Great has been much maligned for killing all those babies in the Bible, and I suppose you have to say fair enough. But don't forget to malign him for the way that he died – a bad case of 'gangrene of the genitals'.

I'm pleased to report that another king, Edward II, had absolutely nothing wrong with *his* genitals. But the same can't be said for his bottom. It's widely believed that this medieval English monarch was murdered by a man wielding a red hot poker. A man who managed to shove said poker straight up the royal rump. ☠

2000s

POLITICAL CORRECTNESS GONE MAD

'They should throw away the key' is a phrase you'll often hear from elderly talkback callers who believe that we're 'too soft on crime'. 'Hanging's too good for them,' 84-year-old Betty will quaver. 'Back in my day, life meant life!' Anything short of a lynch mob tends to enrage these people, the 'revolving door', 'victim-blaming' court system being just another example of 'political correctness gone mad'.

It would be easy to blame the likes of John Laws for all of this, so let's go ahead and do that now.

But urban myth is doing its bit too. A lot of people can tell you for a *fact* that courts punish the innocent, and do their level best to help out the crims. Want an example? Well, they've probably told you for a *fact* that they once knew someone who knew someone, who had a skylight that a burglar once smashed and fell through to the ground. But that's not the best bit, no siree. The best bit was that he then *sued the homeowner* for failing to provide a safe working environment. And, wouldn't you know it, he won.

Equally successful, if urban myth is to be believed, was the criminal who once sued a driver for running him over ... when he was trying to steal hubcaps from the car. Not to mention the woman who sued a nightclub for a having a dangerously high window ... which she fell out of when she was trying to sneak in.

And then there's that young mother who tripped over a toddler in a furniture store and sprained her ankle. She was awarded $780,000 worth of damages by a jury, despite the fact that the toddler was ... well, hers.

Also rolling in the money these days is that woman who had an argument with her boyfriend and threw a drink at him right in a restaurant. Was that restaurant to blame a few minutes later, when she got up from the table and slipped on the floor? A jury apparently decided that the answer was 'yes'.

But the most ludicrous urban legend of all involves a lady whom we shall call Mrs Grazinski. One of those people who probably shouldn't have got a driver's licence – and almost certainly wouldn't have known how to spell it – she supposedly bought a brand-new, nine-metre motorhome in the autumn of 2002. The motorhome had everything a grey nomad could ever want, from a solar-powered fridge and a solar-powered TV, to extra storage and eight hidden beds. It even, she noted with astonishment, had some fandangled new feature called 'cruise control'.

And it was this last feature that she decided to try out, when she started to feel a little fatigued during her very first drive. Hurtling down a freeway at 100 kilometres per hour, Mrs Grazinski calmly got up to make herself a coffee ... in the kitchenette about ten feet away.

It was a rather less calm Mrs Grazinski who then emerged from the wreckage, after her motorhome had flown off the freeway and crashed into a tree. And it was a rather more *wealthy* Mrs Grazinski who later emerged from the courtroom, after suing the makers of the motorhome for not making themselves clear. It's said that she was awarded $1,750,000, along with a brand-new car.

She sounds almost as silly as that man who hurt himself using his lawnmower as a hedge trimmer – and then enriched himself by suing the shop. Though not, perhaps, *quite* as silly as anyone who'd believe any of this. ☻

2000s

BUNDLES OF JOY

When it comes to losing weight, the secret to success is a secret. The world's finest nutritionists have given us liquid diets and low-fat diets, alkaline diets and the Atkins diet. There are experts who suggest we shun calories, and there are experts who say 'eat like a caveman'.

At the end of the day, there's only one thing that we know for sure. This is that if you were to put all the millions of diet books that Australians buy every year on some gigantic, steel-enforced scales, they would probably still weigh less than the average Australian. Obesity is an 'epidemic' in this country, with well over 60 per cent of adults overweight. This stat makes us one of the fattest countries in the entire world (and I'm guessing one of the happiest).

And it's stats like this that make for stories like 'the giant baby' – and make them a little easier to swallow. The brainchild (so to speak) of the *World News Daily Report*, a fake news website par excellence, this urban myth involves a 155-kilogram woman plodding into a Perth hospital and giving birth to an 18-kilogram human.

'I have dealt with other women suffering from obesity before, but this birth will stick with me until I die,' said the doctor who supposedly did the delivery, in the *WNDR* article. 'I truly believed there was two or even three babies in there, but no, it was just one big sturdy guy. He obviously has a career as a future rugby player.'

Not all babies have a future, however: it's time for the story of the Hippy Babysitter. If you've heard it, you may want to turn the page. And the same goes if you haven't.

Still here? Well, then, the story is that a young couple in Wollongong once had a little baby that they both loved very much. But like all parents, John and Mary, as we'll call them, tended to love little Benny a lot more when he was quietly and deeply asleep at home, and they were away in a restaurant or pub. Babysitters are vital to the survival of our species. People just wouldn't have a second child without them, and the human race would slowly wither and die.

Mind you, they need to be *good* babysitters. And it may be fair to say that this particular one wasn't. A sort of drug-addled, bead-wearing bohemian type, with feathers in her hair and a hempen shawl, Rainbow Patchouli Moon Love wasn't exactly John and Mary's *first* choice to mind their precious munchkin, and nor was she their second or third. But when babysitting options four through ten also declined, and they couldn't strike a deal with options eleven to fourteen, the young parents reluctantly signed up the young stoner, with instructions to call them in the event of an emergency.

Rainbow did in fact call them a few hours later, with an emergency case of the munchies. She'd popped a few pills, but had nothing to eat. Was there any way they could help?

'Yes, we can,' said Mary. 'Just wait there, we'll hurry home.' In a panic, the young couple caught a cab straight home – but, alas, they weren't fast enough.

'Yo, bro, peace out,' Rainbow greeted them, her smile ever-so-slightly deranged. 'I've just put that frozen turkey in the oven.'

Unfortunately, John and Mary didn't have a frozen turkey ... and, after that night, they no longer had a child. ☻

2000s

THE CHOICE OF EVERY OTHER GENERATION

Pepsi may well have been 'the choice of a new generation' back in the 1960s and 1970s, but every generation since then has seemed to prefer Coke. Pepsi is essentially what you drink when there's nothing else available in the shop. And you're so dehydrated that you might die of thirst.

Coca-Cola, in other words, simply tastes better – even though, contrary to rumour, it's not liquid cocaine. The idea that Coke is a (very reasonably priced) drug fix has been around since at least the 1920s, only back then it was perfectly true. Invented as a sort of cough syrup (much like another popular medical product, Heroin™), Coke *did* actually contain tiny amounts of nose candy, as a by-product of all its kola nuts and coca leaves. But the recipe has changed a lot since then: it's now coca and kola in name only.

But what exactly did the recipe change *to*? That's the $158 billion question. We are, after all, talking about a drink that some say can cause cancer – not to mention Alzheimer's and kidney disease. We are talking about a drink that you can allegedly use as a cleaning product – or as an aphrodisiac because it contains MSG. A concoction that can dissolve a coin if you place it in a cup overnight, or supposedly explode in your stomach if you drink it with a Mentos.

Common sense tells us that these 'facts' are complete tosh, and Coca-Cola says so too. But the company is not helped by the fact that their recipe remains a trade secret.

Truly? Well, not really. For a start, 99 per cent of the ingredients in Coke are more or less common knowledge. According to a handwritten recipe that's been doing the rounds since the late 1970s, when you slam down a can, you're drinking something like this:

We are talking about a drink that you can allegedly use as a cleaning product – or as an aphrodisiac because it contains MSG.

- Fluid extract of Coca
- Citric acid
- Caffeine
- Sugar
- Water
- Lime juice
- Vanilla
- Caramel

- Alcohol
- Orange oil
- Lemon oil
- Nutmeg oil
- Coriander
- Neroli
- Cinnamon
- 7X flavour

That last ingredient, 7X, makes up about 1 per cent of the can – and 100 per cent of the 'secret'. According to urban legend, only two high-level Coke executives know what goes into 7X, but they each only have half of the story. On no account may these two men or women ever compare notes; in fact, they can't even share the same room.

It seems a strange way to run a $158 billion company. If one of these executives ever has a heart attack, we'll all have to start drinking Pepsi.

The Nazis, of course, would *never* have drunk Pepsi. They were all far too taken by the Coke posters all over 1930s Germany proclaiming 'One People, One Nation, One Drink'. While it would be a bit rich to say that Coke actively *supported* Hitler's regime, urban legend has it that the company had no problems working *with* that regime (at least, until World War II).

The 'Coca-Cola logo rested comfortably next to the swastika' is the view of at least one scholar. He points out that Coca-Cola was the official beverage of the Berlin Olympics, and sent its trucks along to Hitler Youth rallies. And when Hitler marched into Austria, he says, Coca-Cola marched right behind him, quickly setting up a branch in Vienna. According to urban legend, the company convened a meeting in a hall filled with 'gigantic swastikas' to encourage their employees to 'continue the march to success'.

All rather unsavoury. But on the upside, Coca-Cola invented Santa, right? It's often said that the jolly, bearded one's red-and-white robes were directly inspired by Coke's red-and-white cans. And it's true that their December ads throughout the 1930s and 1940s often featured a red-and-white Santa with an icy Coke in hand. There's also no denying that jolly Saint Nick had been getting around in quite a few other colours up until that point, including green, blue and brown.

But it's a stretch to say that it was the Coke ads that created the change: red-and-white Santas predate them by decades. 🎅

SCANDALOUS LEGENDS

'WE ARE ALWAYS READY TO BELIEVE A SCANDAL,' WROTE OVID, THE ANCIENT ROMAN AUTHOR OF THE *METAMORPHOSES*, A 528-PAGE POEM IN DACTYLIC HEXAMETER WHICH I AM HOPING TO NEVER READ.

Two thousand years later, not much has changed. Just as Ovid must have been open to the idea that Julius Caesar was quietly bedding his mum, we are always prepared to believe, well, pretty much *anything*, provided it involves spies, sex or drugs.

Here are some 'scandalous' urban myths. I suspect that they're more entertaining than the *Metamorphoses*.

1788

THE FIRST ORGY

There are many different ways to found a nation, but it's hard to argue that ours was the best. Setting aside fifty thousand years of Indigenous history (and it has to be said that historians are generally happy to), Australia's history as a modern nation state basically kicked off on 26 January 1788, when eleven shiploads of convicts converged on a harbour called Sydney Cove.

Australians tend to regard the First Fleet with a certain fondness – with what you might even call rose-coloured glasses. We see those seven hundred or so convicts as scallywags at worst and as martyrs at best. As desperate, exploited, working-class types who just stole a few loaves of bread. It's probably not true, but none of us much care: some urban myths just aren't worth debunking.

But what about the myth that they were all sex maniacs? I feel like it is my duty to investigate this question, however painful that duty may be. Records show that the First Fleet had 192 women on board, along with a few thousand bottles of rum. It's said that many women were willing to do whatever it took to get a drink, and 'promiscuous intercourse' was the predictable result. 'Their desire ... was so uncontrollable that neither shame ... nor punishment could deter them,' according to the officer in command of the expedition.

116

'There was never a more abandoned set of wretches collected in one place at any period than are now to be met within this ship,' added a surgeon on one of the ships.

Did the good times continue when all eleven ships were finally ashore? Urban legend maintains that on their first night in the new colony, some of the sailors requested an extra ration of rum so they could 'make merry upon the women quitting the ship'. And it would appear that 'make merry' they did. 'It is beyond my abilities to give a just description of the scene of debauchery and riot that ensued during the night,' wrote the surgeon, who was a little judgemental if you ask me. The first boozy party in Australian history saw 'some swearing, others quarrelling, others singing'.

And if the historian Robert Hughes is to be believed, it saw plenty of 'rutting' as well. 'Out came the pannikins, down went the rum, and before long the drunken tars went off to join the convicts in pursuit of the women,' Hughes wrote in *The Fatal Shore*. 'And as the couples rutted between the rocks, guts burning from the harsh Brazilian aguardiente, their clothes slimy with red clay, the sexual history of colonial Australia may fairly be said to have begun'.

Unfortunately, however, the historian Robert Hughes probably *isn't* to be believed. You won't find any reports of a 'foundational orgy' from the year 1788. Or from the year 1789. Or from 1790. In fact, the first person to mention it, Manning Clark, didn't put pen to paper until 1963 and 'after he re-read the sources properly, he quickly re-canted', according to Professor Grace Karskens.

But it was too late to stop the story from spreading. Clark's brief reference to a 'drunken spree' fuelled by 'extra rations of rum' soon became a story of rape, rutting and rolling around in red clay; of 'women floundering to and fro, draggled as muddy chickens under a pump'.

Anyway, that's enough about sex. Let's raise the tone and talk instead about beer. One of the convicts to (not) rut ashore Sydney Cove that day was a London-born thief called Mr James Squire. Transportation did not, alas, signal the end of his thievery, and within twelve months he was hauled before the magistrate, on the charge of stealing a herb from the colony's hospital. This herb was horehound – a plant with a tangy flavour not unlike hops. Squire confessed that he had been brewing beer since his arrival, and selling it for 4d a quart.

The magistrate ordered 150 lashes ... plus two barrels of ale. Australia's first brewery was born.

1892

· · · · · · ·

PARLIAMENT OF WHORES

Australia's 'a sunburnt country', 'a land of sweeping plains'. But there's something that Dorothea Mackellar's poem doesn't tell you: Australia is also a land full of hidden tunnels.

Yep, hidden tunnels. This wide, brown land is more or less riddled with them, if urban legend's to be believed. Sydney, for example, has the Chullora complex: a spacious, steel-lined bunker underneath a block of flats in Marlene Crescent, 15 kilometres west of the CBD. It's said to be full of state of the art military equipment, and connected by an underground tunnel to RAAF Headquarters, just six short kilometres away.

If you take a spade over to the other side of the country, you might just find an underground tunnel linking Perth's Supreme Court building to its Old Mint, out in the east. And if you've ever wondered why that city doesn't have an underground rail system, the answer is that it almost did. The story goes that builders began to make one in the 1920s, only to stop when they found 'strange cyclopean tunnels'.

Adelaide, for its part, has secret tunnels connecting its Parliament House to its Government House, and the headquarters of General Motors Holden to an RAAF base.

And don't feel neglected, Brisbanites. You have a hidden tunnel under Boggo Road Gaol. It supposedly snakes its way through Dutton Park and Annerley, ending up at the old Lord Alfred Hotel.

But the grand champion in this area is undoubtedly Melbourne, a city so criss-crossed with underground caverns it's a wonder it hasn't collapsed. Apart from all the World War II bomb shelters scattered around Port Melbourne, and that train tunnel to the airport that some still insist was half-built,

No culprit was ever found. But that didn't stop fingers being pointed in the direction of Madame Brussels, a woman who knew what to do with a stick.

there are all of gangster Squizzy Taylor's hideaways underneath Richmond, and that big tunnel that connects St Leonard's College to Haileybury. Plus all those big bunkers full of World War II military equipment in Clifton Hill. And/or Northcote. And/or the Dandenongs. And that massive aircraft hangar hidden somewhere near Spencer Street.

But why bother going to any of these places when you could just whip your pants off and check out a brothel? Australia's most scandalous mythical tunnel is the one that supposedly connected the Victorian Parliament of the 1890s to a den of vice just down the road. Located in Little Lonsdale Street (which was, in the words of the disapproving evangelist Henry Varley, 'a loathsome centre in which crime, gambling hells, opium dens and degraded Chinese abound'), this comparatively high-class 'gentleman's club' was the place where politicians went out to play. Our tax dollars bought it a little bell that rang whenever Parliament was getting ready to vote, and one of Victoria's only private phones.

Now that's customer service, my friends, and the woman who provided it was a real-life actual person called 'Madame Brussels'. Named after her nipples (which were so big they were like 'Brussels sprouts'), this procuress was described at the time as a 'magnificent pink, white and golden-maned animal' who held high society in the palm of her hand. We're told she 'was always well-dressed,' she 'drove in a smart carriage' and she 'educated her daughter at a respectable private school'. Sure, some people called her 'the Queen of Evil', or 'that fecund field in female form', but Madame Brussels had plenty of friends in high places (and had probably shagged them all).

But even *they* couldn't protect Madame from the rumour mill when Victoria's Parliamentary Mace went missing. A long silver stick that sits beside the speaker and shines forth with an ancient symbolism, the mace in a Westminster Parliament represents its fundamental right to exist. It's an enduring emblem of Western democracy. It's one of those things that you try not to mislay.

But mislay it someone did. An unsolved mystery to this very day, the (still-missing) mace was almost certainly stolen, but no culprit was ever found. That didn't stop fingers being pointed in the direction of Madame Brussels, a woman who knew what to do with a stick. Urban legend maintains that the mace was taken, via underground tunnel, to her bordello, by a group of drunken politicians who were up for a laugh.

As to what else they were up for, it's not hard to speculate. Sounds rather painful, but each to their own.

1967

HAROLD HOLT, CHINESE SPY

Would you trust your son or daughter to the Charles Manson Childcare Centre? Or the Dr Philip H Nitschke Hospital? It would be a bit like sending them to a playground named after Evel Knievel, or a restaurant named The Salmonella Express.

The good news is that none of these places exist. But there *is* a Harold Holt Swim Centre. Designed in a style that architects call 'brutalist' (and that everyone else calls 'extremely ugly'), this grey concrete swimming pool got its name from a prime minister who was so good at swimming he drowned.

A resident of the Lodge for just twenty-two months, Harold Holt is now best remembered for that day in December 1967 when he took a few friends to Port Phillip Bay and decided to take a quick little dip. They urged him not to be stupid – Cheviot Beach is basically one big deathtrap, with jagged rocks, rough waves and strong rips – but, being the prime minister who had just sent more troops to Vietnam, Holt was clearly someone who could ignore good advice. He dived into the water, instantly disappeared from view, and to this day he's not been seen since.

Or has he? If one urban myth is to be believed, parents should not be worrying about *drowning* when they drop their kids off at the Harold Holt Swim Centre. They should be worried that their child is a spy. The story goes that Holt – an accomplished skindiver, with 'incredible powers of endurance underwater' – was in fact a spy for Communist China, Australia's sworn foe during the Cold War. By late 1967, he had become worried that his cover was about to be blown, and decided to leave Australia for the People's Republic. So his red paymasters sent along a submarine to Port Phillip, and ever so subtly helped him give us the slip.

That's certainly one theory, anyway. Though a better theory is that this is crap. 'Harry? Chinese submarine?' his widow, Dame Zara Holt, said years later. 'He didn't even like Chinese cooking.' The spy story seems to have begun with a 1970s novelist called Anthony Grey who, in his defence, seemed to 'sincerely believe' it. But he was also a man who sincerely believed in UFOs. The spy legend has been denounced as a 'complete fabrication' by every one of Holt's many biographers.

And they also give short shrift to crackpot theory two: that Holt was in fact killed by the CIA, because he was planning to wind back Australia's involvement in Vietnam. Not least because he wasn't. A staunchly conservative leader of the Liberal Party, Holt was an enthusiastic Cold War warrior.

So let's just scrap the murder idea. What about suicide? Perhaps a little more plausible is crackpot theory three: that the PM had tired of life. He was certainly struggling in the polls at the time of his death, and staring down a potential leadership challenge from Treasurer Billy McMahon.

One Cabinet colleague insists that Holt was so 'depressed' by his former friend's treachery that he was at the stage where 'he just didn't care'. And some reports say that he had been using 'a cocktail of prescription drugs, including morphine' to treat a nasty shoulder injury, 'which may have impaired his judgement on that fateful day'.

'Il n'est pas impossible,' as the French might say, if they had any idea who Harold Holt was. But the problem is that Holt had *always* been a crazy-brave swimmer – right from childhood, he was reckless to the point of idiocy when it came to dangerous rocks, waves and rips. Most serious commentators – and, indeed, the Victorian Coroner – are satisfied that Holt was in a perfectly ordinary state of mind at the time of his death. 'Now, if somebody is planning to jump off a cliff, they are not at the same time planning to have a major cabinet review of the direction that Australia's taking,' is how Malcolm Fraser put it. Later a prime minster himself, Fraser said that he and Holt had several long discussions about the future of Australian foreign policy in the days before Holt disappeared.

'And if anyone had challenged Harold in a leadership contest, he [Holt] would have won it in a canter. There is absolutely nothing new [when it comes to long-discredited allegations of suicide, murder or escape]. So why rehash the memory?'

Sorry, Malcolm. I'll stop now.

1969

· · · · · · · · · · ·

ONE SMALL FIB FOR MAN

If we can send a man to the moon, why have we not sent a woman? Is it just because the moon doesn't need cleaning?

Sorry, terrible joke, that. You, the reader, deserve so much more. But it does at least help me to raise the question: did America *actually* send a man to the moon? Because if Neil Armstrong's 'giant leap for mankind' was really a giant *hoax* on mankind, as so many conspiracy theorists continually insist, then it was a hoax that all Australians can be proud of.

As depicted in the Sam Neil film *The Dish,* and some SBS documentary that was a bit long and dull, you might recall that it was an *Australian* telescope (the Parkes Observatory in central New South Wales) that received the video footage of the Apollo 11 astronauts all the way from the moon, and fed it to TV screens all over the globe. If the moon landing was all just a big piece of theatre, then it was Aussie scientists who helped set the stage.

The hoax theory goes that, after Soviet cosmonaut Yuri Gagarin became the first man in space, the US became desperate to send the first man to the moon. Anything went in the 'space race,' played out as it was during the ideological pissing contest that historians call the Cold War. But despite spending tens of billions of dollars and subcontracting something in the order of four hundred thousand people, the good folk at NASA just couldn't get the job done (the moon being quite a long way away).

How much more sensible, someone decided, to just build a film set – so up one went in the Hollywood Hills. That famous footage of Neil Armstrong & Co was merely a shorter and less-well-acted version of *2001: A Space Odyssey*, the Stanley Kubrick film shot a year before.

A good urban legend, but could it be accurate? Well, the most oft-cited piece of 'evidence' is the US flag that the astronauts patriotically stuck in the ground. Check it out on YouTube and you'll see it flutter. The moon, of course, ought to be a flutter-free zone. The fact that it doesn't have an atmosphere also means that it doesn't have wind.

Proof number two relates to what you *can't* see. Stars. Shouldn't there be at least a few in the background?

The third piece of 'evidence', if you don't mind my using that term, relates to the shadows that the astronauts give off. Each of them differs wildly in length, despite there being just one source of light (the sun). Or were there actually multiple sources of light, the 'moon' being a film set and all?

Convinced? You really shouldn't be. Look again at that flag and you'll see that it only flutters when the astronaut is *planting it into the ground*. Other than that, it's completely still. (And it's worth noting that the dust he kicks up while he fiddles with the flag doesn't gather into little floating clouds

The good folk at NASA just couldn't get the job done (the moon being quite a long way away).

like it would back on Earth. It just falls straight back down to the ground, as you would expect in outer space.)

As to the absence of stars, that's another thing that you might expect, given that the moon landing took place during the lunar daytime. The sun is shining straight onto the surface and blocking out the (less bright) distant stars. It's no different to daytime down here on Earth. It's not that stars *disappear* in the morning – we just can't see them because the sky is too bright.

And why did that sun produce different-length shadows? The answer is simply that the moon has an uneven surface.

But at the end of the day, the most compelling argument against a hoax is that the four hundred thousand people who would have all been involved in some way have all managed to keep silent for some forty-odd years. Wouldn't at least *one* of them have fessed up on *Oprah* by now, or sold their story to the *News of the World*?

So the 'fake landing' is just an urban legend. But it's far from my favourite about NASA. It's said that, after that organisation had finally sent a few men into space, it began grappling with a more mundane problem. Ordinary pens won't work in zero gravity, and they're also affected by outer space's extreme temperatures. So NASA scientists supposedly spent thousands of hours and over $12 billion developing a pen that was immune to gravity and able to function in extreme cold and heat.

The Russians just used a pencil.

1975

· · · · · · · · · · ·

SIR JOHN KERR, CIA STOOGE

If some conspiracy theories are to be believed, there's barely a country anywhere in the world whose government doesn't in some way owe its existence to the US of A. With their dark sunglasses and dark-grey suits, state-of-the-art gadgets and shiny guns, CIA agents are simply *everywhere* in South America, and also busy pulling strings in the Middle East. African governments, of course, are really just *American* governments: locally made puppets with an acceptably black face. And if you've ever been under the impression that Asian people actually run Asia, then you clearly haven't read John le Carré.

But what about the Australian government? The CIA may well have backed and financed murderous despots in Chile, Haiti, Iran and the Congo, but surely even *they* would draw the line at Tony Abbott?

Well, maybe. But Malcolm Fraser could be a different story, according to one enduring urban myth. The story starts with Sir John Kerr, the man Gough Whitlam appointed Australia's governor-general after he was sensationally swept to power in 1972, following decades of conservative government. Once on board the ship of state, Whitlam instantly swung the wheel left. It took the radical new PM about a day to end Australia's involvement in Vietnam and to establish a relationship with Communist China. And it only took a few weeks for his ministers to condemn the US government as 'corrupt and barbaric', and privately demand to know what the CIA was really getting up to at Pine Gap, the top-secret 'Joint Defence Space Research Facility' that the former Liberal Government had allowed it to build somewhere near Alice Springs.

'We were told that the Australians might as well be regarded as North Vietnamese collaborators', says former CIA analyst Frank Snepp, while two of his colleagues have admitted off the record that 'the Whitlam problem' was viewed 'with urgency' by the CIA's then director, William Colby, and that 'arrangements' were made.

Was one of these 'arrangements' Sir John Kerr's dismissal of the Whitlam government in November 1975? Arguably the most important event in Australian political history, it certainly remains the most controversial. 'Well may we say "God save the Queen"', as Whitlam famously put it, 'because nothing will save the Governor-General.'

Did the CIA ask Kerr to do it? *Pay* him to do it? *Order* him to do it? *Force* him to do it?

If you ask me, the answer is 'probably not', but all I have to go on is common sense. For conspiracy theorists with a thousand hours' Googling behind them (hours that have also revealed how September 11 was an 'inside job' and the Boxing Day tsunami was really a bomb), it seems very clear that Kerr was a spy.

For one thing, he had 'long-standing ties to Anglo-American intelligence'. A distinguished judge and lawyer (with a sideline in heavy drinking), Kerr spent World War II working for the Directorate of Research and Civil Affairs, a mysterious Australian army think tank about which almost nothing is known. He was also an 'enthusiastic member' of the Australian Association for Cultural Freedom: 'an elite, invitation-only group ... founded, funded and generally run by the CIA'.

'The CIA paid for Kerr's travel, built his prestige and even published his writings through a subsidised magazine,' claims former agent Victor Marchetti. He also maintains that yet another organisation that Kerr was associated with, LawAsia, 'often served as a cover for clandestine operations'.

Whether or not all *that's* true, we do know that, feeling 'pissed off because their cover as far as Pine Gap was concerned was blown', the CIA did threaten to withdraw intelligence cooperation from Australia – and that this was a threat that was conveyed to Kerr just three days before the dismissal. 'I don't think [the threat] was decisive,' said Whitlam's former defence minister in 2000, 'but I think it reinforced his position [about the dismissal]. Kerr loved the cloak and dagger.'

Yes, well, don't we all ... ⚔

1980s

HIJINKS AT THE LOGIES

'Loathsome'. 'Noxious'. 'Harrowing'. 'Vile'. These are all pretty strong words.

But are any of them quite strong enough to describe the Logies? Australian television's 'night of nights' should really be classified as torture under some UN convention. Viewers are subjected to speeches and sequins, and starlets with spray tans; we see botox and endless fake boobs. Then there're all the top-shelf talent like Brynne Edelsten arm in arm with ~~bogans~~ contestants from *My Kitchen Rules* and *The Block*. It's like watching everything that's wrong with Western civilisation while getting repeatedly stabbed.

But nothing in this world is *all* bad. (Well, at least not since *Being Lara Bingle* was axed). If nothing else, the Logies are at least a good source of scurrilous rumours: they're a sort of urban myth factory with way too much make-up, and people who say 'Darling' a lot. In contrast to the Emmys and the Academy Awards (two famously 'dry' events), the organisers of the Logies don't so much *allow* alcohol as actively *encourage* it, plying the stick-thin, crash-dieting starlets with champagne and chardonnay from around about 4pm. 'There's a saying in the industry that people who attend the

Logies always get really drunk at their first one,' says one industry insider. 'It's quite a stressful night for the publicists, trying to keep the talent tidy.'

And all the coke floating around wouldn't really help. 'I've seen more drug-taking at Logies parties than I've seen on the road in rock'n'roll bands,' says musician James Reyne. 'I've seen some people that are well-known talking heads on Australian television who are so respected ... taking drugs in the cubicles.'

'Attending the Logies, you pick up more dirt than any top-brand vacuum cleaner,' agrees Jeanne Little, who brought home a gold statue during the 1970s. 'You see people's behaviour behind the scenes.'

So, who's done what? Well, tempting as it is to name names here, there's also something very appealing about not getting sued. All I can say is that one actress may not have been available to accept her Logie because she was otherwise engaged in the toilet, while another one may now regret sucking off adadsflasdf in the foyer for all to see. And something that rhymes with 'sucking' apparently went on in the elevator one year, in a scene involving a former host of ███████████████████. If you don't believe me, you should try to check out the security footage that was leaked to the internet. I believe that many people have.

There's also that urban legend about the soapie star who clambered on top of a table right in the middle of the telecast, then whipped off her undies and started to dance. Though *she* was still relatively well-dressed compared to the Channel 7 personality who supposedly sat in Isaac Hayes's hotel suite stark naked, waiting for the special-guest crooner to open the door.

We should also note that ███████ ███████ was fully and properly clothed when he was rushed off to hospital during a Logies party, after dabbling in a cocktail of drugs.

So ... are there any names that we *can* name? Well, it's said that the actor who played Mr Big in *Sex and the City* was more like 'Mr Sleaze' when he came to the Logies. Another 'international guest star,' *Friends* actor Matt LeBlanc, was allegedly not so much friendly as 'rude', while George Eads of *CSI* fame was not so much rude as actively obnoxious. But the worst Logies guest of all time was Raquel Welch, if urban legend is to be believed. It's said the '60s sexpot only turned up to the event at the eleventh hour,

If nothing else, the Logies are at least a good source of scurrilous rumours: they're a sort of urban myth factory with way too much make-up, and people who say 'Darling' a lot.

135

and then immediately announced she would leave again unless someone made this squalid little affair worth her while. Channel 7 boss Christopher Skase had to hand over $20,000 worth of jewellery before she condescended to go on the red carpet.

But it's worth noting that, for all her supposed haughtiness, Welch never won an Oscar. Unlike Marisa Tomei. My all-time-favourite awards show rumour (apart from the one that Channel ■ rorted the votes for the 19■ Logies by buying 20,000 copies of *TV Week*) is that Tomei's Best Actress Oscar for *My Cousin Vinny* was actually intended for somebody else. Legend insists that the award was meant to go to Vanessa Redgrave for her turn in *Howard's End*, but that 'drunk or stoned' Oscar presenter Jack Palance was too drunk or stoned to read the cue card properly.

I suspect that this rumour is total crap. But hey, so are awards ceremonies. 🥂

1980s

• •   • • • •   • •

BEDROOM SHENANIGANS

'Don't have sex, man,' Steve Martin once advised. 'It leads to kissing and pretty soon you have to start talking to them.'

Sensible words, Señor Martin, but so many of us seem to ignore them. Take that famous AFL footballer who turned up to a journalist's house for an interview ... only to have her open the door entirely naked, save for thigh-high leather boots. I am not talking about the journalist who was caught having sex in a news chopper, here, but the one who later went on to have an affair with a rock star – one that resulted in a quick trip to hospital so that a broken champagne bottle (or Coke bottle or Vegemite jar) could be carefully extracted from deep within her arse.

Sorry, this is all very sordid. And sexist and almost certainly untrue. But people have been making up sex stories about celebrities for years: take that empress of Russia, Catherine the Great, who supposedly died while having sex with a horse. Or the Roman Emperor Caligula, who knocked up his sister. Albert Einstein supposedly slept with so many women, it's a wonder that he found time to do science.

Rod Stewart is said to have had similar habits, way back in his 1970s heyday. One of the internet's more ridiculous urban myths insists that the Scotsman once needed to stop a concert halfway through, so he could go have his stomach pumped in hospital. The problem, apparently, was that he'd spent the previous night with some sailors and swallowed way too much of their semen. Stewart, who says he's 'as heterosexual as they come', blames a former employee for starting the story. 'I used to have this guy work for me, he was a gay publicist ... I had to fire him because he did something terrible, which I won't go into. He wanted revenge so he started this rumour about me, and it was horrible because my kids were at school. So that is definitely not true.'

Not every celebrity can be called 'as heterosexual as they come', however. Urban legend insists that Abraham Lincoln was gay, along with Richard Nixon and J Edgar Hoover. And Marlon Brando and Cary Grant and James Dean.

Dozens of popes are said to have joined them in the closet – but, when it comes to expressing yourself in the bedroom, it has to be said that a pope called Benedict IX needs a cupboard of his own. Described by historian Ferdinand Gregorovius as 'a demon from hell in the disguise of a priest', Benedict was, according to one of his successors, a man 'so foul, so execrable that I shudder to think of it'. He was frequently accused of bestiality, though with which animal his accusers never made clear.

As we all know, Richard Gere prefers gerbils. (Though let's be clear that by 'we', I really mean *you*.) The silver-maned star is far from the first celebrity to have endured rumours about a late-night visit to an emergency ward, so he could have a small creature removed from his arse. (According to most accounts, the gerbil didn't make it. It seems like a pretty bad way to go.) Much the same story has done the rounds about a well-known American gridiron player and a TV presenter on the East Coast.

Gere's turn came after theirs, in the early 1990s, following the worldwide success of *Pretty Woman*. A still-anonymous prankster faxed all over the world a copy of a letter 'from' the American Society for the Prevention of Cruelty to Animals that attacked the actor for 'gerbil abuse'. A lie can travel halfway around the world while the truth is still putting its pants on, as Mark Twain or someone like that once said. Over the following decade, we all discovered that we knew someone who knew someone who knew someone, who knew someone who was in the hospital at the time.

1990

CANDID CAMERA

Monogamy, as some wag once put it, leaves a great deal to be desired. Researchers have found that about 40 per cent of people admit to straying on their partner in thought, word or deed, and about 60 per cent of people are liars.

In an ideal world, of course, nobody would cheat: our love would shine through in all that we do, and we would think, act and feel with integrity. (Or maybe everybody would cheat but no one would ever get caught. Yes, let's aim for that.)

It's difficult to imagine a world where getting caught cheating is ever good – let alone getting caught on TV. But it was just such a fate that befell the 'cheating couple of London Bridge', if urban legend is to be believed. The London Bridge of this story is not the actual structure that spans the Thames in the capital of England, but a big, old rock off the Great Ocean Road. A 200-foot-high, sort of upside-down U that (if you had bad eyesight) kind of looked like a bridge, London Bridge was a popular stopping point for carsick sightseers who weren't feeling all that picky after a 300-kilometre drive.

Said sightseers would get out of their car, walk on top of the 'bridge' and think wistful thoughts about their Melbourne hotels.

But in January 1990, everything changed. Just like in the nursery rhyme, London Bridge started falling down, as the horizontal bit that connected the two vertical clumps of rock began to crack and collapse. Within a few seconds, London Bridge had finished falling down, leaving a husband and a wife utterly stranded on clump two ... right in the middle of the rough, choppy ocean.

It wasn't just a dangerous situation, but also an awkward one. Because, for all that this man and woman were legally married, the woman and the man that they were married to were actually elsewhere ...

The good news is that the cheating couple were eventually rescued by a helicopter from emergency services. The bad news is that it arrived quite a while after the Channel 9 helicopter, and the ones from Channels 7, 10 and 2. There were also a few dozen journos and newspaper photographers waiting to greet them when they finally made it onto shore.

Sadly that story isn't totally true. While two people *were* left stranded when London Bridge collapsed, they weren't a cheating couple – they were cousins, and they had another friend waiting for them in the car.

But even if it had been true, there may well be even worse ways to be caught in the act. Let's turn our attention to another urban myth. It features a middle-aged woman who lived all by herself but for Rufus, her big, pet dog. One day, the story goes, the unnamed lady's unnamed friends decided to throw a surprise party for her fiftieth birthday, and so snaffled a key to her two-storey house. Ever so quietly, so as not to disturb the dog, a dozen of them snuck into her bedroom, clutching champagne, candles and cake. And ever so quietly they waited, while the door opened downstairs.

But five minutes passed, and she didn't come up, and then ten minutes passed after that. After twenty minutes, they decided to seize the bull by the horns (or, less metaphorically, to softly tread down the stairs). 'SURPRISE!' the friends yelled, swinging open the kitchen door – and they were right, there were surprises all round. The unnamed woman was surprised to see them. And they were surprised to see her lying on the floor. Entirely naked. Except for some peanut butter in the crotch region. Which Rufus was busy licking away.

1990s

NOT RECOMMENDED FOR CHILDREN

'Are you thinking what I'm thinking, B1?'

'I think I am, B2.'

So goes every second conversation between those two fruity, yellow icons of Australian television, a Channel 2 fixture for almost four decades. But what exactly was the ABC thinking when it decided to put bananas in pyjamas?

The answer is clearly penises, if you subscribe to the urban myth. Specifically, erect penises first thing in the morning, or erect penises that are wearing a condom. Why the man who wrote the song that inspired the show (Carey Blyton, the British nephew of Enid) should have believed that erect penises come 'down the stairs', and then 'chase teddy bears', has never really been made clear, but hey, it takes all types. Perhaps it's something to do with the way they 'come down in pairs'?

Still more confusingly, it's also considered 'obvious' by those in the know that the 'B' in B1 and B2 stands for 'buggery'. That caught me unawares.

143

Urban myth may be a bit more reliable when it comes to the adventures of Captain Horatio Pugwash. After all, his crew contained a first mate by the name of 'Master Bates' and a sailor called 'Seaman Staines'. And, if either of them failed, he could always 'Roger the Cabin Boy'.

Only he couldn't. The *Captain Pugwash* cartoon, which first ran on the BBC in the 1960s, actually had an entendre-free cast. There was a Master *Mate* aboard, together with a *Tom* the Cabin Boy, and absolutely no semen stains in sight. The seedy myth came about after a tongue-in-cheek magazine article, the authors of which ended up in court.

But more seedy myths are not hard to find. Even Disney – sweet, innocent Disney, that multinational mass-media corporation with diversified stock holdings and a heart of gold – has been said to peddle in smut. In *The Little Mermaid*, for example, some point out that, when the bishop marries the sea witch to the dashing Prince Eric, he does so with quite a bulge in his pants.

And teenage boys might get a bulge themselves when they watch *Who Framed Roger Rabbit*. They just need to pause that scene where Jessica Rabbit is in a car crash and flies through the air, long legs akimbo. Squint a bit while holding a magnifying glass, and it begins to seem possible that a creepy cartoonist somehow forgot to draw her some undies.

Maybe this guy also helped draw *Aladdin*? There's a scene in the Robin Williams classic when our hero comes face to face with a growling tiger, and stammers something like, 'Good kitty ... take off and go.' Or that's what the script says, anyway. Urban legend insists that Aladdin actually says something different – something like, 'Good teenagers, take off your clothes.'

But maybe Disney is just following tradition? If you believe 'common knowledge' about nursery rhymes, after all, smut has been getting smuggled into kids' stuff for quite some time. According to some sources, the Jack and Jill of, well, 'Jack and Jill', were actually having sex when they were up on that hill: to 'lose your crown' is to lose your virginity.

And it's hard to see how 'Goosey Goosey Gander' would have hung on to *her* virginity if it's true that 'goose' was slang for a prostitute.

And what about that 'Marjorie Daw' who liked to 'see-saw'? According to the London scholar Chris Roberts, she was a 'filthy slut' who decided to 'sell her bed and lay on muck'. Which is just charming, I'm sure you'll agree.

1990s

MYTHS, DRUGS AND ROCK'N'ROLL

Music and drugs are like bacon and eggs, a successful and time-honoured team. But what about *children*'s music and drugs? Should *they* go together? Without wanting to be in any way judgemental, it seems, well ... I don't know ... wrong. Children should probably be protected from that stuff until they can get to university and start doing it properly.

Luckily the issue doesn't really arise. Unless you want to believe urban myth. Some punters, for example, insist that the Wiggles' anthem 'Wake up, Jeff' actually dates back to the group's days as the Cockroaches, a rock band in the late 1980s. It's said that keyboardist Jeff Fatt – now better known as the Purple Wiggle – enjoyed the occasional toot and, as a result, kept falling asleep.

But (let's be clear here, lawyers) it's not said by me. The 'Stoner Jeff' idea originated in a joke magazine article that compared the Wiggles to the Beatles – a joke that clearly flew over one reader's head. As clean-cut as his purple skivvy would suggest, Fatt is actually a power-napper from way back. 'He really does fall asleep,' says former Yellow Wiggle, Greg, of the man whose 'laid-back personality' always made him 'invaluable company on the road'.

But not everyone spends their time on the road, of course. 'Puff, the Magic Dragon', for example, preferred to live by the sea, spending a lot of time frolicking in 'Autumn mist' and being visited by a young boy named 'Little Jackie Paper'.

Does this mean that Jackie was a dope head? People in the know have always 'known' that 'Puff, the Magic Dragon' is a song about taking a puff on a joint. And who could ever doubt that 'dragon' means 'dragging', 'Jackie Paper' means 'rolling papers' and that an 'autumn mist' is a drug-induced haze?

Anyone who knows the songwriter, that's who. Folk musician Peter Yarrow got the lyrics from a poem that his college roommate wrote way back in 1959 – a poem which was in turn inspired by an Ogden Nash rhyme. 'Puff is about loss of innocence,' Yarrow has maintained to this day, 'and having to face an adult world. It's surely not about drugs. I can tell you that at Cornell in 1959, no one smoked grass. I find that fact that people interpret it as a drug song annoying. It would be insidious to propagandise about drugs in a song for little kids.'

Yes, it would, I say to John Lennon, he who wrote 'Lucy in the Sky with Diamonds'. But, whatever 'those in the know' might tell you about that strange, psychedelic concoction of 'tangerine trees', 'marmalade skies' and 'plasticine porters with looking glass ties', Lennon always maintained that 'LSD' was not actually a song about LSD. 'It never was, and nobody believes me. I swear to God, or swear to Mao, or to anybody you like, I had no idea it spelled LSD. This is the truth: My son came home with a drawing

147

and showed me this strange-looking woman flying around. I said, "What is it?" and he said, "It's Lucy in the sky with diamonds," and I thought, *That's beautiful.*

'The images were from *Alice in Wonderland*. It was Alice in the boat. She is buying an egg and it turns into Humpty-Dumpty. The woman serving in the shop turns into a sheep, and the next minute they're rowing in a boat somewhere – and I was visualising that. There was also the image of the female who would someday come to save me – a "girl with kaleidoscope eyes" who would come out of the sky. It's not an acid song.'

Convinced? Well, if Lennon was lying he was certainly a little bit better at it than Joe Cocker. The gravelly-voiced rocker who famously covered 'With a Little Help from My Friends' may have actually needed a *lot* of help from pretty much everybody, if this urban myth is anything to go by. The story is that, sometime in the 1970s, Joe was enjoying himself in an Adelaide hotel suite with a little help from a big fat joint. As tragically uncool then as they are to this day, the South Australian Drug Squad suddenly burst through the door, uninvited, and demanded to know where he'd stashed the dope.

Joe blinked a bit, frowned a bit, and gazed about the room, his brain needing a little while to wake up and swing into action. Finally, he gave up and shrugged his shoulders. 'There's some around here somewhere.'

1990s

THE MCDONALD'S '100% AUSTRALIAN' LIE

Working at McDonald's can teach you a lot about life. The key lesson is that it's not always worth living. What's really the point of getting up in the morning if you have to put on a stripy top and tight white hairnet? At McDonald's, you learn about eight-hour shifts and what life is like on a miserly wage. You discover how working at the fryer can cause all sorts of acne, and exactly how rude hungry, fat men can be.

But one thing that you *don't* learn at McDonald's is how to keep a big secret all to yourself. A lot of bad things are said about Australia's favourite fast-food giant, and a small portion of them are actually untrue.

Urban myth number one: that the '100% Australian beef' McDonald's always lists as an ingredient is not really Australian at all. '100% Australian beef' is just the name of a company that sells Macca's patties from somewhere very cheap overseas.

Myth two: that it's not even 100% *beef*. McDonald's patties are actually made up of worm meat, possibly mixed up with a few eyeballs and a sprinkling of sawdust and bones.

Myth three concerns McDonald's thickshakes – which some say are not called *milk*shakes for a very good reason. The truth, however, is that they *do* actually have a splash of milk in them (along with nutritious additives like stabiliser 452, vegetable gum 407 and acidity regulator 330). And you won't find any pig fat in a McDonald's soft serve, or any petroleum in their French fries.

You will find plenty of sugar, synthetic chemicals and trans fats on the McDonald's menu, along with what could be the promise of an early death.

Still, you will find plenty of sugar, synthetic chemicals and trans fats on the McDonald's menu, along with what could be the promise of an early death. It's certainly not a myth that the company's food is unhealthy and a great way to start building a gut.

Given this, you'd think that people would have been grateful to Robert Trugabe – but for some reason his reputation is bad. Almost anyone with access to the internet has seen Mr Trugabe's 'confidential memo' at some point in their life. In it, this 'senior manager' of McDonald's Australia suggests that staff should be instructed to leave out a little bit of food from 'every second or third' drive-through order, while of course still charging full price.

> We need to discuss the drive-through orders as well [the ~~Zimbabwean dictator~~ manager writes]. If the girls leave one item out of every second or third order, this adds up to several thousand dollars per week revenue. On smaller orders if they leave out the hot apple pie or fires [sic] and larger orders just 1 burger from every third order this totals around $2,118.00 per day. We need to work out if there is a way of making this a procedure without making it documented.

A good point, well made, but not perhaps all that ethical? Robert Trugabe would have been in a great deal of trouble if it wasn't for the fact that he didn't exist. McDonald's has since published the following 'customer alert' on its website:

> The memo in circulation online and via email supposedly written by the Managing Director/Proprietor of Frewville McDonald's in South Australia is a complete fabrication. 'Robert Trugabe' is not nor has ever been a McDonald's Australia employee. The contents of the letter are also completely fabricated. McDonald's practices the highest standards of consumer ethics and would never encourage employees to act in a way that undermines our core customer values.

KFC, of course, also has its core customer values. One of the most important ones (if PETA is to be believed) is that it is okay to 'cram birds into huge waste-filled factories, breed and drug them to grow so large that they can't even walk, and often break their wings and legs'.

But perhaps claims of systematic, shit-strewn cruelty are a bit overblown? After all, many say that the real reason 'KFC' is no longer called 'Kentucky Fried Chicken' is because it no longer serves chickens at all. As one typical viral email puts it:

> *They actually use genetically manipulated organisms. These so called 'chickens' are kept alive by tubes inserted into their bodies to pump blood and nutrients throughout their structure. They have no beaks, no feathers, and no feet. Their bone structure is dramatically shrunk to get more meat out of them. This is great for KFC because they do not have to pay so much for their production costs. There is no more plucking of the feathers or the removal of the beaks and feet.*

Come to think of it, that sounds even crueller. Thankfully, it's entirely untrue.

1990s

· · · · · · · · ·

BUYERS BEWARE

Religion is dying in this brisk, modern world, along with old-fashioned values and norms. Words like 'honour' and 'duty' are fast losing importance, and who really cares about their family and friends?

Where, then, can we find meaning in life? What exactly is the point of it all?

The answer, of course, is buying stuff. People who lack a sense of purpose in life clearly haven't watched enough ads. Oh what a feeling you'll get if you buy a Toyota, and you ought to be congratulated if you buy MeadowLea. It's lucky if you're with AAMI, and Brand Power will help you buy better. And while a hard-earned thirst needs a big cold beer, and the best cold beer is Vic, we should also note that Red Bull gives you wings, Berocca gives you bounce, and a large range of soft drinks can boast Schweppervesence.

But are multinational corporations really the moral beacons we all know them to be? Or might some of those urban myths you hear actually be true? Let's examine the allegations one at a time.

Allegation one: Adidas. Now, this shoe company's runners may promote 'mid-foot integrity', plus 'energy-harnessing stretch web outsoles' which 'stretch with your foot strike', but is that any excuse to get sexual? Adidas may well have been founded by a German man whose name was Adi Dassler, but urban legend insists that 'Adidas' is actually an acronym. It stands for 'All day long I dream about sex'.

The founder of Marlboro, on the other hand, apparently spent his days dreaming about white supremacy. Despite the fact that Philip Morris was a small-time tobacconist who worked near Greater Malborough Street, London, urban myth insists that he was a member of the Ku Klux Klan and used his company's profits to take down the blacks. The basis for this opinion seems to be that a red-and-white packet of Marlboros, turned on its side, looks more or less like the letter K. And ... well ... that's it. The prosecution rests, your honour.

Tommy Hilfiger was rather less subtle in *his* defence of the Master Race. According to urban myth, that fashion designer once went on *Oprah* and announced he'd rather Asians and black people buy other clothes. I'd suggest that you check out the footage on YouTube, but the problem is that he never said anything like that, which made the footage quite hard to tape.

Racism is more than just horrible, of course – as we all know, it's silly as well. Apart from anything else, to see the world in terms of black and white is to ignore the fact that we all have red spots. From acne and eczema, to scabies and shingles, we're all human, and we all have skin problems. And, if you believe an urban myth, we can all use the same cure. Windex will cure just about any skin disease, say people on the internet (and you can believe them because they're not doctors).

Prevention, however, is even better than cure – and you'll be glad to know that Vegemite prevents mosquito bites. The soft drink Mountain Dew, on the other hand, will prevent you from having a baby (if you believe the internet rather than all those so-called 'scientists'). Despite looking, smelling and tasting just like an ordinary lemonade, and being made of the exact same ingredients, it supposedly has a mysterious ability to reduce a man's sperm count.

Scientists also suggest that we ignore people who say that Spam is actually the favourite food of certain Pacific Islanders because it tastes not unlike human flesh. (It's popular in the Pacific because importing fresh meat is far too expensive.) I myself ate some 'spiced ham' quite recently and it actually tastes not unlike crap.

For the *real* taste of human flesh, you could take a nibble out of John Tanner, an elderly Melbourne man who was run over by a steam-roller in 1910. Urban myth has it that Steam Rollers mints were rather tackily inspired by said event.

It's just a pity that Chinese Pepsi wasn't around at the time. Perhaps John's descendants could travel to China now. Urban myth has it that one of the soft drink company's famous slogans reads a little differently in the worker's paradise. In China, you don't just 'Come alive with the Pepsi Generation'. Pepsi actually 'brings your ancestors back from the grave'.

SPORTY LEGENDS

WHETHER OR NOT SPORT IS OUR 'NATIONAL RELIGION', IT'S NO SECRET THAT AUSSIES LOVE THEIR SPORT (OR, AT LEAST, THINK IT'S OKAY). REGARDLESS OF RACE, RELIGION, CLASS, GENDER OR CREED, SPORT BRINGS PEOPLE TOGETHER, AND THEN DIVIDES THEM UP INTO WINNERS AND LOSERS.

But, with obesity levels at an all-time high, and diabetes on the rise, how many Australians actually love *playing* sport, as opposed to just (drinking and) watching it? In my case, sport may be one of the reasons I get up on the weekend, but I generally just head to the TV room and then collapse, out of breath, on the couch.

It's a bit of a myth that we're a nation of super-athletes – a place of fit, bronzed and active outdoors types, who are all itching to take a crack at the Poms. And it would seem that the sport myths don't stop there ...

1850s

AFL, THE INDIGENOUS GAME

'You have your way. I have my way,' said the German philosopher Frederick Nietzsche. 'As for the right way, the correct way, and the only way, it does not exist.'

While it's worth noting that Nietzsche ended up in an insane asylum, I think we can all agree that these words make sense. Open-mindedness is *everything* in a modern liberal democracy; mere 'tolerance' isn't nearly enough. Whether we're talking about sexuality or gender or race or religion, or people who post weekly photos of their children on Facebook, the things that make us different are all things that we should celebrate – they are the engines that make society hum.

There is, however, one exception to this 'open-mindedness' rule. I am, of course, talking about people who don't like AFL. While there's a school of thought that says they just need education and counselling, I say that we need to get tough and throw them in jail. AFL, after all, is *our* sport: a home-grown game that's unlike any other. Enjoying Aussie Rules should be a patriotic duty, along with making nasty comments about Gina Rinehart and ordering beer when you'd really prefer riesling.

The game was invented by a 19th-century sportsman whom some called 'the finest cricketer of the age'. Raised in rural Victoria, just north of the Grampians, and educated in the UK, Tom Wills was captain of the Rugby School cricket team and represented Cambridge in their match against Oxford. The athletic all-rounder went on to play first-class cricket for a few seasons in Kent, before returning to Australia in 1856 to help run the new Melbourne Cricket Club.

A couple of years into his reign, however, Wills noticed something that's still pretty true: much like seals, and certain other aquatic mammals, cricketers tend to get pretty fat in winter. Some sort of exercise was clearly needed to keep off the pounds, so Wills went out and invented a sport. With his cousin and a couple of others, he sat down with some beers, came up with some Aussie rules, and a whole new style of football was born.

Unfortunately, Wills went on sinking beers. The sportsman became a serious alcoholic – one who eventually killed himself by plunging a pair of scissors into his chest.

It's a tragic story with a big missing chapter: where did Wills get his ideas for the laws of Aussie football? His experiences at Rugby School obviously had something to do with it: England's private schools all liked to play their own private sports, a habit which has given the world 'Winchester Football' and Eton's 'Field Game', and, rather more famously, rugby itself.

But could the rest of the answer lie in Tom Wills's childhood years, spent on a wool farm at the foot of the Grampians? It's certainly true that he was close friends with many of the Aboriginal kids in the area, and frequently joined in their pastimes and games. Could one of those activities have been Marn

Grook, a football-like game that was often played at Indigenous gatherings, with a ball made from possum skin? Like Pultja and Wotjoballuk (two not dissimilar sports played further north), Marn Grook involved lots of distinctively AFL features, like drop punts, free kicks and high marks.

But was it actually played in the Grampians? Unfortunately, the answer's probably 'no'. Official AFL historian Gillian Hibbins says it's a 'seductive myth' that Wills was exposed to the game as a kid: Marn Grook was actually played hundreds of miles to the south.

'Understandably, the appealing idea that Australian football is a truly Australian native game recognising the indigenous people, rather than deriving solely from a colonial dependence upon the British background, has been uncritically embraced and accepted in some places,' Hibbins writes.

'Sadly, this emotional belief lacks any intellectual credibility.' ⚽

1861

ARCHER'S EPIC WALK

There's something very special about the first Tuesday in November. And I'm not talking about the fact that it is invariably followed by the first Wednesday in November, and then the first Thursday the day after that. While this is no doubt impressive – a record of steady, consistent achievement that only six other weekdays could match – I'm actually thinking of something more impressive still.

'Tis this. Every first Tuesday in November sees every second person in Victoria suddenly acquire an interest in horseracing. People who knew next to nothing about horses, and who were only dimly aware that they raced, will suddenly start to use words like 'furlong', 'plunge', 'lock' and 'lay'. The Melbourne Cup is the race that stops (about one-fifth of) the nation – and then, thank Christ, we can all move on.

A two-mile run for three-year-olds, held in front of 100,000-plus people at Flemington, Australia's richest horserace is also one of our oldest. It kicked off in 1861, at the height of the gold rush, and weather-wise, everything went according to plan: 'A more propitious day, it would have been difficult to realise,' reported *The Age*, and 'the Grand Stand was tolerably well-filled'. Spectacle-wise, however, it was a disaster. The crowd witnessed a race in which three horses crashed into a white picket fence, with two of them later put down. A fourth horse bolted off the course, and the winning time of three minutes and fifty-two seconds remains the slowest winning time to this day. Also, *The Age* was lying. The Grand Stand was practically empty.

And worst of all, the winning horse came from New South Wales. The Melbourne Cup was supposed to be a showcase for Melbourne – a city whose inferiority complex when it comes to Sydney is ... well ... probably justified.

That winning horse was, of course, Archer – and he's also the subject of a big urban myth. If you believe that godawful 1980s movie, *Archer's Adventure*, which stars a young Nicole Kidman before she learnt how to act, Archer *walked* all the way to Flemington from a stable in Nowra, New South Wales. That's a seven hundred kilometre-long journey. A journey through dust, rocks, heat and rain. That's roughly 699.5 kilometres longer than I'm prepared to walk anywhere, unless there's some form of alcohol at journey's end.

Is there any truth to the story (which has been around for at least 150 years)? Well, there was certainly no rail link between Nowra and Melbourne back in 1861, which is probably the reason why the legend began. But the problem is that there were plenty of steamships – and plenty of evidence to show that this is how the thoroughbred travelled. Take this 21 September 1861 clipping from *Bell's Sporting Chronicle*:

Wednesday last saw the departure of [Archer trainer] Mr De Mestre's three nags for Melbourne, and by this time we trust they have arrived in good order. A large number of friends went down to the wharf to see the horses on board, and we may safely say that wishes for the successful issue of the trip are very general.

Or this entry, two weeks later:

The City of Sydney, which reached Sandridge (Port Melbourne) on Saturday last brought the Sydney entries for the Melbourne Cup, viz, Archer, Inheritor and Exeter. Archer is considered the best old good 'un in New South Wales. The horses reached this colony without a scratch, and remained at Kirk's Bazaar until Wednesday, when they took up their abode at the Botanical Hotel, South Yarra.

So, the story of the stallion with extraordinary stamina seems to be just that – a big, fat story. You should not see *Archer's Adventure* as a piece of history.

In fact, as someone who's sat through it, my advice is not to see it at all. ☻

1882

THE ASHES ARE A BURNT CRICKET BAIL

As the world's best tennis players walk into centre court at Wimbledon, they see a couple of lines from a poem by Rudyard Kipling inscribed just above the big oak doors: 'If you can meet with Triumph and Disaster / And treat those two impostors just the same ...' The message here, of course, is that winning isn't everything. It's more important to be a good person, than it is to be a person who's good at a sport.

And this message is, of course, horse shit. Life is not a 'journey', children; it's a race which you don't want to lose. When your mum said that 'winning isn't everything', what she really meant was that you also need to collect prize money and a big, silver trophy to flaunt in front of your friends.

A little clay trophy can also be good, provided it contains the remains of a burnt cricket bail. Just eleven centimetres tall, all covered in cracks, and with home-made handles that are slightly skewiff, the Ashes urn may have

begun life as a bottle of perfume, but it's now one of the world's great prizes. It's up there with a Tour de France jersey or an Olympic gold medal, or this absolutely superb meat tray that I once won in a raffle. It's a time-honoured terracotta symbol of a cricket rivalry that's still without peer.

But what are they ashes *of*, exactly? Could the whole burnt cricket bail thing be a big urban myth? Let's examine the facts.

The story of the Ashes begins in 1882, when the Colony of Australia sent a team to the Mother Country to give English people more of a chance to make jokes about convicts. The English weren't laughing when we won a Test at The Oval, though. Or, rather, they *were*, but it was at themselves. Mock obituaries appeared in a number of newspapers, the most famous being this one, which was published in *The Sporting Times*:

> In Affectionate Remembrance of English Cricket, which died at The Oval on 29th August 1882. Deeply lamented by a large circle of sorrowing friends and acquaintance. RIP. The body will be cremated and the ashes taken to Australia.

When England sent a team of its own to Australia a year later, its captain joked to journalists that his goal was to 'take back the ashes'. And take them back, Ivo Bligh did: his team won two tests to one in December, but the ashes were still just a metaphor.

Things changed over Christmas, however, while the team enjoyed a short holiday at Rupertswood, a plush mansion in rural Victoria. The story goes that, to commemorate their guests' win (and help pass the time because there was no TV), the team's host, Lady Janet Clarke, and her friend Florence Morphy decided that it would be fun to make the metaphor real.

So they symbolically cremated a cricket bail, and looked around for an appropriate vessel.

The pair eventually found an old perfume bottle which more or less looked like an urn if you closed your eyes. They put the bail's ashes inside and presented it to Bligh over lunch, wrapped up in a red velvet bag. Toasts were made, laughs were had, and a timeless sporting tradition was born.

But is the tradition based on the truth? In 1998, Morphy's 82-year-old daughter-in-law said that her mother and Clarke actually burnt a *veil*, not a bail – crepe being more flammable than wood.

We'll probably never know, but it probably doesn't matter. Because another legend has it that, decades later, when the urn was sitting on Ivo Bligh's mantelpiece, a clumsy servant knocked it all over the floor. Have you ever tried getting ash out of carpet? The servant didn't. He just replaced it with a bit of ash from the fireplace.

And Australia and England have been competing for a bit of burnt log ever since. ⚽

1894

TOP SHOT

There are a great many myths about cricket – e.g. that it's entertaining to watch. I don't mean to disparage a game in which next to nothing happens for five long days, because, clearly, there is no need to. Watching cricket is like watching grass grow after taking a sleeping pill, and then hitting yourself on the head with a mallet. It's a wonderful reason to get up off the couch and change the channel to a different sport.

But perhaps I am being unfair here. While cricket doesn't have all that much to offer when it comes to, well, almost anything, it is at least a great source of urban myths. Did you know, for example, that Nazi Germany had its own cricket team, until Hitler had everyone killed? Or that the Admiral Nelson of Trafalgar Square fame actually lost his eye to a nasty bouncer? It's also worth noting that, while Pakistan often loses to India, they've won every One Day match the teams have played on a Friday. Also, I can reveal that whenever a team reached the score of 111, the umpire David Shepherd liked to stand on one leg.

Don't worry if you haven't heard any of these things – it's the sign of a life well spent. (Plus, they are not true.) But even *you* should really have heard the one about the batsman who hit 286 runs off a ball. 'Rubbish!'

you reply with a scepticism that I must say becomes you well. 'The first-class record for runs scored off one ball belongs to one Albert Hornby of Lancashire Cricket Club, thanks to a few sloppy overthrows, and the ball being temporarily mislaid in long grass. But he just scored a sensible ten.'

'True enough,' I respond, silently marvelling at your mastery of detail, but that's just *first-class* cricket. Tales abound in the lower levels about big scores that were hit off one ball. Take this story from the *Pall Mall Gazette*, for example, which is dated 15 January 1894:

> *Western Australia is advancing rapidly, but it seems to be still a little behind in the matter of scientific cricket. A match was recently played at Bonbury, Western Australia, between the Victorian team and a scratch XI from the neighbourhood. The 'gumsuckers' went in first, and the first ball bowled was skied into a three-pronged branch of a tall jarrah tree. The home team cried 'lost ball', but the umpire ruled that as it was in sight it could not be lost. The Victorians started running, while the West Australians sent for an axe to cut down the tree. No axe being obtainable, somebody brought out a rifle, and the ball, after numerous misses, was shot down. The score on the one hit was 286, and the Victorians 'stood' [declared] on that, and put the other side in. The Victorians won.*

True story or total crap? Well, as Michael Jones points out on the ESPN Cricinfo website, there was actually no coverage of this supposed incident in any *Australian* newspapers, which is a little odd, given that that's where it 'happened'. The closest we can come to one is an article in Perth's *Western Mail*. Written months later, it refers to the story as 'that enormous fairy tale

... A hit for 286 licks all cricket creation, using the word in its imaginary sense, of course.'

Okay, total crap then. ⚽

1932

WHY DID PHAR LAP DIE?

Melbourne Museum has a great many exhibits that are well worth giving a miss. If you haven't seen its special 'Rainforest Gallery', then please make sure that you never do. I have, and, believe me, it sucks.

But there are diamonds in there, amid the dross, and the best one is in the shape of a horse. For 'tis at Melbourne Museum that one can see Phar Lap, or at least what remains of his eyes, skin and fur. The greatest racehorse in history (if you exclude Secretariat and Seabiscuit and Man O'War ... and Black Caviar and Ruffian and Frankel), Phar Lap captured Australia's imagination during the dark days of the 1930s – a time when people were so poor they didn't so much consider *selling* their kidneys, as cooking them up for a nice, hot meal. The Depression was deeply depressing, and all who lived through it really needed a lift.

And they got one in the form of Phar Lap, an awkward-looking, over-sized chestnut colt who was bought for just 130 guineas. A gangly klutz who kept tripping over during training and finished last in his very first race.

But it's fair to say that he improved. Between 1929 and 1932, Phar Lap snaffled a Melbourne Cup, two Cox Plates and an AJC Derby, amid thirty-seven wins from fifty-two starts. His biggest win of all was North America's richest race, the Agua Caliente Handicap, which he took out in a track-record time.

But the Agua Caliente wasn't just the triumphant exclamation mark to an amazing career. It also became the full stop. Because just two weeks after that famous race, the five-year-old colt suddenly came down with a high temperature at his stable in San Francisco: he haemorrhaged for a few hours, and never got up.

So what happened? Was there foul play? To this day, nobody really knows. Two comprehensive official autopsies and countless analyses from all sorts of scientists have essentially concluded that the cause of death could have been just about anything. It could have been feed that had been sprayed with insecticide. It could have been something to do with bacteria called 'duodenitis-proximal jejunitis'.

Or it might simply have been murder. Ask anyone in the know, and they'll point the finger at gangsters. And it's true that the continued success of 'the Australian wonder horse' probably wouldn't have been wonderful news for at least one or two of America's bookmakers – men who rarely got confused with choir boys, but who might have easily been mistaken for criminals. Adding fuel (or, rather, deadly poison) to the fire is the fact that a scientific analysis of Phar Lap's hide a few years ago found tell-tale traces of arsenic.

But *what* tale do these traces tell, exactly? Arsenic was actually a not-uncommon (and not illegal) 'stimulant' back in the 1920s and 1930s. It was a standard ingredient of health-giving tonics, like strychnine and belladonna and coke. Could Phar Lap's trainers just have been trying to put a little more pep in his step, but accidentally got the dose a bit wrong?

Maybe. Or maybe not, if you believe Big Red's beloved strapper. Tommy Woodcock once briefly touched on the matter of 'tonics' in a newspaper interview and said that he always refused to use them on his champion racehorse, despite repeated

So what happened? Was there foul play? To this day, nobody really knows.

orders from his boss. 'At first I used to argue that a horse like Phar Lap did not want a tonic, but as time went on I adopted tactics. To please [part-owner, Harry] Telford I would take the bottle, but would pour a quantity down the drain each day so that he would think that I was carrying out his instructions.'

'Given the legendary nature of Phar Lap's story, it is probably impossible to convince anybody to change their minds as to the cause of death,' says one of the horse's biographers, 'but surely Woodcock's comments in 1936 in *The Mercury* are hard to dispute. Unless we are prepared to say that

Tommy Woodcock was a downright liar, which even today, decades after the loveable and respected horseman's death, would ostracise us with the Australian racing public, we must accept him on his word. The ineluctable conclusion we are left with, whether we like it or not, is that Phar Lap's impeccable achievements here and overseas were utterly tonic, stimulant and drug free.'

The ineluctable conclusion that *I* am left with? It's that anyone who tells you that they know who or what killed Phar Lap is telling you an urban myth. ✪

1948

A TEARY FAREWELL

Much like our former prime minister, Kevin Rudd, Don Bradman was a man whose biggest fans seem to have been people who never met him. Aloof to the point of unfriendliness – and fond of money to the point of greed – the Don was far from a bad man, but he certainly wasn't one of the boys. 'Bradman was a chap who found it terribly hard to mix with the hoi polloi', said teammate Bill O'Reilly. 'He never made the slightest effort to be a real 100 per cent team man.'

'He certainly lacked empathy', is how one biographer of this 'extremely peculiar Australian' puts it, 'and had a near obsessional ability to concentrate intensely for long periods on repetitive tasks.'

Could it be that Bradman was a little autistic? That the single-minded perfectionism that made him such a champion batsman – such a clinical, focused competitor; such a relentless accumulator of runs – also made him a man with slightly *blah* people skills? A man who didn't attend the funerals of his parents or four elder siblings, and who went through life with just a handful of friends? A man whose activities as a stockbroker raised quite a few eyebrows? And a sportsman who was 'invalided' out of World War II, before going on to lead the Invincibles?

174

Who really knows? All we *do* know is that Bradman *was* invincible. Put a bat in his hand and the Boy from Bowral could hit just about any ball for a four. The second-best batting average in the history of cricket belongs to South Africa's Graeme Pollock. His twenty-three matches yielded him 2256 runs, at an average of just over sixty. Our Don, in contrast, had an average of *99.94*. It's a record so far above and beyond that of every other batsman that they may as well have just played chess. And it's a record, as so many statisticians have pointed out, that sits above and beyond any other in sport: 99.94 is the equivalent of a basketballer averaging fifty points a game, or a soccer player scoring one goal per match. It's equivalent to somebody breakdancing on a tightrope without hands, feet or eyes, while undergoing heart surgery and juggling six lions. It just doesn't happen.

And his average could have been better still. One of the game's great tragedies for people who hadn't met Bradman – and great treats for people who had – was that the Don didn't finish his career averaging exactly one hundred. After all, he got so very close. When the forty-year-old walked out to bat in the fifth test at The Oval, for the final time in his illustrious career, he brought an average of 101.39 to the crease. Everyone knew that he just needed to score four more runs to cap off a magnificent and unique career in a unique and magnificent way. He was greeted with a standing ovation from the crowd and three cheers from the English fielders. He had a flat pitch and a clear blue sky. The stage was set for history to be made. All he had to do was just say his four lines.

Instead he said something like, 'Oops', after being bowled for a second-ball duck. (Two of his teammates didn't say anything, because they were too busy having a fit of the giggles. 'I thought they were going to have a stroke, they were laughing so much,' reported a BBC commentator later on.)

Should we get to the urban myth bit? It probably seems like it's just about time. Legend has it that Bradman was deceived by Eric Hollies' 'perfect length googly' because he was batting with a tear in his eye. It's an idea that started straightaway, thanks to John Arlott, the radio commentator. 'What does one say under these circumstances?' he pondered aloud on air. 'I wonder if you see the ball very clearly in your last Test in England, on a ground where you've played some of the biggest cricket in your life; and where the opposing side has just stood round you and given you three cheers; and the crowd has clapped you all the way to the wicket. I wonder if you see the ball at all.'

The Don's opponents didn't wonder, however. 'That bugger Bradman never had a tear in his eye in his whole life,' is how one of the slip fielders put it.

Anyway, we'll never know – just as we'll never know what Bradman's average might have been if he was playing today. The story goes that, sometime in or around 1990, he was asked for his thoughts on that very question: How did the Don think he might go against the likes of Marshall and Garner?

'Oh, I reckon I'd average fifty or sixty,' he replied.

'But you averaged nearly a hundred in your career, and you played some of the great bowlers in history,' said the reporter, with some surprise.

'Well, yes,' said Bradman. 'But you've got to remember that I'm eighty-two years old now.' ☢

1989

THE BOONIE AND THE BEER

Averages, scores, records, statistics ... cricket is a game of numbers. Any fan who's worth their salt knows that Muttiah Muralitharan took 800 test wickets throughout the course of his career, and that Courtney Walsh once got 519. Bradman's batting average is carved in every cricket lover's brain, and we can all remember where we were when Mark Taylor retired on 334.

But for the true purist, one stat stands alone – in fact, it stands as a symbol for all that's great about sport. I am, of course, talking about David Boon's famous feat of drinking fifty-two beers on the long flight to England, as part of his special training for the 1989 Ashes. It's a stat which says that you don't have to be tall, slim and fit to be a top-level sportsman (though, to be honest, that generally helps). It's a stat that says you can do it and still drink enough alcohol to kill a small warthog – and, well, kind of look like one too.

But perhaps it's not actually a stat? Could the 'fifty-two' figure just be a big urban myth? That's what the man himself would have us believe: 'Never

But for the true purist, one stat stands alone ... I am, of course, talking about David Boon's famous feat of drinking fifty-two beers on the long flight to England.

spoken about it, never will,' is all Boonie will say whenever he's asked about the legendary booze-up (as he still is about three times a day). 'I know there are plenty of stories flying around about me that have been greatly embellished over the years, but that's how it is ... We played our cricket in an era where blokes learned never to let the truth get in the way of a good story.'

He also played in an era when big, hairy blokes with enormous moustaches did this kind of thing all the time. The tradition of getting on a plane massively pissed, and then getting even more pissed for the next twenty hours, seems to have begun back in 1973, when the Australian team flew back from a tour of the Caribbean. According to Doug Walters, Rod Marsh turned to him and asked, '"How many cans do you think we'll have before we get to Sydney?" I said, "twenty-five." He said, "It's a thirty hour flight – we'll have thirty-five."' The pair set about testing this hypothesis, but encountered a problem after ten hours' research. The plane ran out of beer.

Not to be deterred, the fearless fact-finders decided to resume their experiment the next time the team flew to England. And this time, the boys all joined in. Bets were laid, rules were agreed on, and almighty hangovers were born. Walters was the eventual winner, having downed forty-four cans by the time they hit Heathrow. He celebrated by lighting his cigarette filter and taking a deep drag from the other end.

And so matters stood until the Age of Boon – which unfortunately was also supposed to be a new age of fitness. Australia's coach Bob Simpson had sought to introduce a new professionalism into his moustachioed troops; broadly speaking, this meant occasional push-ups and a great deal less time on the piss. The team had just been thrashed by the Windies, so the flight to England for a six-match Ashes series probably wasn't the best time for a laugh and a spew.

'Boonie never set out with the intention of breaking the record,' recalls teammate Dean Jones, 'but not long into the flight, the Qantas staff advised us that they'd been keeping count, and Boonie was well on target.'

Eight hours later, it's said that the portly opener polished off can number fifty-two (or fifty-five, if you count the three in the flight lounge). Jones, who'd been sleeping off his effort, says that he woke up to 'tumultuous applause'. 'Then the captain of the plane got on to the PA system and congratulated Boonie on his fantastic effort of breaking the record.'

Supposedly 'purple with anger', Simpson called a team meeting not long after landing. 'Righto,' he fumed, 'a couple of things: David, I'm very disappointed with you and you're on probation, but also I don't want this story to leave this room. It's not to leave the Australian cricket team.'

As Jones later recalled, an awkward silence followed, which Merv Hughes broke by putting his hand up. 'He went, "Oh, Bob, I'm sorry, mate, I've done radio interviews with ..." and he named four or five stations he'd done interviews with, and said, "Mate, it's all over the world."' ⚽

1990s

BOXERS WHO BOXED ON

'Champions,' said Muhammad Ali, 'aren't made in the gym. Champions are made from something they have deep inside them.'

The 'something' he's referring to, of course, is a violent streak. To be able to float like a butterfly, sting like a bee and happily incur brain damage from repeated blows to the head, it really helps to have a bit of a temper. A temper so short that it's measured in millimetres, and knuckles that feel all lonely when there's no one to punch. The list of boxers who've been in prison is as long as Mike Tyson's arm (though less muscly and tattooed).

And then there's the list of boxers who maybe *should* have gone to prison, if urban myth is to be believed. Take Australia's own Jeff Fenech, for example – a man who used to love youse all. We were 'the most beautifullest people in the world' back in the 1980s and early 1990s, when the Marrickville Mauler was the world champ. But by 1999, we'd become 'a jealous, sick race of people who do not want to give credit when others have done something good'. 'Jealousy is worse than cancer,' Jeff complained. 'Jealousy is worse than AIDS.'

Essentially, Jeff had a problem with rumourmongers – those who may not have wanted to credit him with ever doing something good, but who were always happy to say something bad. Stories abound about the little Aussie battler, which as a writer who'd rather not get sued (or shot), I have bravely decided not to repeat.

But I'm sure that Jeff won't mind my bringing up the story about a time in Atlantic City when a less-than-polite, 100-kilogram bouncer supposedly stood between him and a nightclub door. One punch later, however, the bouncer was *lying* between him and the door. Fenech may have been a featherweight, but he's a hard man to push around.

So, for that matter, is convicted rapist Mike Tyson – a man who probably doesn't like being called a 'convicted rapist', but who also doesn't know where I live. Like Fenech, Iron Mike is said to have had one or two scuffles outside the ring (by which we mean one or two hundred). The most notorious (supposed) scuffle was with Wesley Snipes, Hollywood star of *Money Train* and the *Blade* trilogy. The story goes that Tyson was in a nightclub one evening, when he saw his girlfriend sitting on the (bad) actor's lap. 'He chased her away and then took Snipes into the men's room where he proceeded to lay a beat down on the pleading movie star,' says an internet 'source'. 'By the time Tyson was done with him, Snipes was snoring on the floor.'

There was, however, very little snoring whenever Jack Johnson did his thing in the ring. The southern-born son of two former slaves, the first black World Heavyweight Champion (who won the title in 1908) ought to have been keeping people awake with his lightning-quick footwork, sneaky right jab and thumping left hook. But some spectators hardly noticed these things ... being too distracted by his great, big dick. Urban myth maintains that (perhaps in response to racist rumours that he was a shameless 'seducer of white women'), Johnson used to wrap his little buddy up in bandages 'to enhance its size ... and flaunt his genetic endowments for all to admire'.

But however many bandages he may have shoved down his pants, Johnson's johnson was certainly not as big as the most famous boat that sank in the sea. The *Titanic* was one big ship (until it became one big shipwreck). Another urban myth insists that the boxer actually tried to buy a ticket for the liner's first (and last) voyage, but was denied a berth because of his race.

The list of boxers who've been in prison is s long as Mike Tyson's arm (though less muscly and tattooed).

Anyway, that's enough penis talk. Because Johnson also had some pretty big balls. Another urban legend (from long before the Civil Rights era) says that the boxer was once driving along a southern road very fast in his sports car, when he was pulled over by a big white cop. Said cop gave him a $50 speeding ticket and a few serves of the n-word to boot. But while $50 was a lot of money at the time, it wasn't so much if you were the heavyweight champ: Johnson simply fished out a crisp $100 note from a big wallet full of them, and handed it over, mid-racist tirade.

'How the fuck am I supposed to give you change?' the surprised copper responded.

'Don't worry, you can keep it. I'm planning to drive back this way, and I'm going to go pretty fast.' ⚽

1995

THUGBY

Did you know that badminton was invented at Badminton House, the home of the Dukes of Beaufort? And that the Earl of Derby, the man who invented the Derby, used to live at a house called The Oaks?

Of course you did, I never doubted you for a moment: apologies all round. Both houses, as it happens, are just a few miles from another ancient haunt of sporty aristocrats: the ever-so-exclusive Rugby School. It would go without saying that rugby was invented there, but that's no way to write a book.

In 1823, so the story goes, assorted students were playing a game of soccer when one of them – a certain William Webb Ellis – accidentally caught an airborne ball. But instead of dropping it so that the other team could take a penalty kick, and bracing himself for an evening of sexually charged bullying, the blighter went and ran with the thing, all the way to his own team's goal. 'With what result as to the game I know not,' wrote another student in 1876, 'neither do I know how this infringement of a well-known rule was followed up, or when it became, as it is now, a standing rule.' All the writer did know was that a new game had been born.

And all we know is that this is all crap. The story of William Webb Ellis didn't 'come to light' until years after his death. It came from a man who

185

had never met him and who got the story from an unnamed source. An 1895 investigation by the Old Rugbeian Society was 'unable to procure any first-hand evidence of the occurrence' (or any good reason why there should be an 'Old Rugbeian Society'). It's true enough that the game began at the school, but we'll never know how (or why).

I don't, as you may have gathered by now, have a lot of time for either league or union. (Though the one game that I watched seemed to last for about six weeks. As a spectacle, it was a bit like having a lobotomy, only more painful and not as fun.)

But I'll admit that there are some good rugby urban myths.

Take the 1995 World Cup, for example, a tournament that Australia sadly lost in the Quarters. Happily, however, we got to see New Zealand claw its way into the final against host nation South Africa – and then meet with a thudding defeat. The match had kicked off with a spectacular air show: helicopters and fighter jets flying overhead, and skydivers plummeting down to the ground, plumes of coloured smoke coming out of their boots. But could that smoke have been (as has been suggested by the odd disappointed Kiwi) some sort of toxic gas? A cunning trick to enfeeble the All Blacks?

Well, no. Not unless you're the sort of person who also believes that South Africa had already dispatched 'a young woman from Bloemfontein' a few days earlier to distract one of New Zealand's star players with her sexual arts. Or that the country somehow arranged to have half the New Zealand team get food poisoning two days before the final. 'It was just an amazing sequence of events and coincidence that, of our 35-man party that ate at

186

that particular lunch venue in the hotel here, about twenty-seven of them went down in the space of twelve hours,' said the New Zealand coach much later. 'You can read what you like into that, but I don't think it was coincidence. We certainly have our suspicions ... I don't have any doubt that it left many of them pretty flat, and I think that was a significant factor in us just not quite having the urgency and speed in our game.'

If the entire Welsh team falls ill in the next few years, I for one will suspect the Pope. An urban legend says that whenever Wales wins European rugby's 'grand slam' – that is to say, beats England, Scotland, Ireland and France in a single year – a pope dies.

It's not quite true, but it's not quite false. Of the eight Roman Catholic pontiffs who have died since international rugby began, five expired in a year when Wales won the Slam.

Coincidence? God knows. ⚽

1999

THE DAY SOUTH AFRICA DROPPED THE WORLD CUP

It's the moment every Australian remembers. (So long as they like cricket ... And have a reasonable memory ... And, I guess, were watching the game at the time.) The World Cup Cricket quarter final. Australia vs South Africa. Headingley, 1999. The Aussies bat second, having been set the big target of 271, and find themselves in big trouble early on. But cometh the hour, cometh the bloke: Steve Waugh walks to the crease with the score at three for forty-eight, and proceeds to peel off 120 from 110 balls. Wickets fall all around him. But Australia still wins with two balls to spare. And then go on to win the World Cup.

But that's not even the best bit. Also known as 'Tugga' and 'Ice-Man' (and as the only person in the known universe who likes that John Williamson song 'True Blue'), Waugh's nickname should really be 'Oscar Wilde'. Because when he was on fifty-six during that glorious game, and then spooned an easy catch which was dropped at mid-off, our true blue captain had a gold-

standard sledge – and he fired it off within 1.2 seconds. 'You just dropped the World Cup,' he taunted the unfortunate fielder, Herschelle Gibbs. And if that's not Wilde-like, then what the hell is?

Except, of course, he didn't say that. The whole story's just a big urban myth. Waugh's always admitted that he 'wasn't quite that clever. I wish I could claim that, and the myth is sort of perpetuated and I'm going to break it a bit but it wasn't quite that, I just said: "Look, do you realise you've just cost your team the game."'

'Tis not an unusual story: 'Misquotations are often stickier than actual quotes,' as Abraham Lincoln once said. History is full of wonderful lines that people from history never actually said.

Julius Caesar's final words, for example, weren't *'Et tu, Brute'*; they were probably something like 'Ouch'. Those three words just happen to form his final line in the Shakespeare play, when the Brutus character gets out a knife. The same goes for 'A horse, a horse, my kingdom for a horse.' That's just more solid scriptwriting in Willie's *Richard III*.

Any other mythical final lines? Well, Ned Kelly never said 'Such is life' before putting his head in a noose. The phrase was just the last line in a newspaper article about his hanging – one that concluded with his actual last line ('Ah, well, I suppose it had to come to this') and then threw in a little bit more.

Hanging would have been too good for Stalin, a man who said that, while one death could be seen as a tragedy, 'one million deaths is just a statistic': we should have made him sit through *The Bachelor*. But while he clearly thought something along these lines, it also seems clear that he never actually said it. The quote comes from a satirical essay by a German pacifist.

No one ever accused Machiavelli of pacifism. The author of *The Prince* was a man who preferred the stick to the carrot. (Unless that carrot could somehow be poisoned, and then placed in an enemy's soup.) But he never said that 'the ends justify the means'. That's just some academic's snappy summary of his work.

The same story applies to Darwin's immortal phrase 'the survival of the fittest', and Voltaire's equally famous defence of free speech. 'I disapprove of what you say, but I will defend to the death your right to say it,' said some academic, not Voltaire.

Our true blue captain had a gold-standard sledge – and he fired it off within 1.2 seconds.

Mythical quotes are also popular in popular culture – most often thanks to the movies. Phrases like 'Elementary, my dear Watson' and 'I vant to suck your blood' never came from the creators of Sherlock and Dracula. They just popped up in much-later movies, and for whatever reason stuck in our minds.

And then we have lines like 'Play it again, Sam' and 'Beam me up, Scotty'. Only we don't actually have them at all. Watch *Casablanca* and *Star Trek* as many times as you like, but you won't ever hear them said. Equally, you can read as much Sigmund Freud as you like, but you won't discover that 'a cigar is sometimes just a cigar'. Just like the rest of us, Freud knew perfectly well that a cigar is a penis. ⚽

2000s

HE COULDA BEEN A CONTENDER

Everybody knows a coulda-been champion – a one-time sportsman or woman who 'could have been anything' were it not for some cruel twist of fate. Only, let's be honest, they're generally a man. A fat, boozy, chain-smoking man who also maintains that today's [insert sport] has 'gone to the dogs'. You'll see them on every second golf course, or bullying their children at the under-age footy.

And then we have the coulda-been *another type of* champion: those men and women who *did* in fact excel at their chosen sport, X, but who could have mastered sport Y or Z instead. Like the AFL footballer Todd Viney, who was a promising tennis player in his younger days. Such a promising player, urban legend says, that he once beat a young Boris Becker.

Among the many other AFL players who 'could have been anything', we have the West Coast Eagle Nic Naitanui (Olympic high jumper) and his former teammate Ben Cousins (world-class triathlete). Hawthorn's Jarryd Roughead could have been an NBA basketballer, just like Collingwood's captain Scott Pendlebury and power forward Jesse White. Former number

192

one draft picks Luke Hodge and Brett Deledio could have 'easily' pursued careers in first-class cricket, while the world of golf missed out on a major gun when Jeff White chose to play AFL.

Shane Warne, as it happens, also chose to pursue AFL, but the game was just a little too quick. He played with the St Kilda under 19s, before spinning off into a different sport. Two of his former teammates could also kick a ball, though in their case that ball was round. Steve and Mark Waugh represented New South Wales in soccer and tennis – and Don Bradman could have been brilliant at squash.

Rafael Nadal and Roger Federer also excel at tennis, but their soccer skills are not quite as well-known. Both men could have been pros, it's widely thought. Though not necessarily by people who know them.

Steffi Graf, however, was an even more super athlete, if an urban legend from the Seoul Olympics has a grain of truth. It's said that, while she was staying in the Athlete's Village as part of the (extremely good) West German team, that tennis star decided to train with some 800-metre runners, just to pass the time and have a bit of a laugh. Without even warming up, the story goes, she circled the track twice in such a good time that she would have qualified for that year's final.

Usain Bolt, of course, can run faster still, provided the distance is one or two hundred metres. But the Jamaican maintains that his *true* sporting talent is actually soccer. So talented is the sprinter, in fact, that he could be a real help to Manchester United. 'I am a very accomplished player and know I could make a difference,' Bolt announced to the press, not long after the London Olympics. 'I would be the fastest player in the team, but

I can play as well. If Alex Ferguson wants to give me a call, he knows where I am.'

We also know where Michael Jordan is – and that is, a town called *regret*. His Airness was the world's most famous sportsman throughout the 1980s and '90s, and took this fact to mean that he could play any sport. The greatest basketballer to ever play the game famously gave it away when he hit thirty-one in order to play a sport at which he'd starred as a child. Jordan signed a minor league baseball contract with the Chicago White Sox, with a view to eventually making the majors.

'It took a lot of guts to retire when he did,' said his agent, David Falk. 'It took a lot of guts to go play baseball and run the risk of failure after being incredibly successful at something else. But Michael is fearless.'

This may be true, but he's not great at baseball. Jordan returned to the Chicago Bulls in 1994, after a thirteen-month stint in the minor leagues that *Sports Illustrated* described as 'embarrassing'.

Sometimes it's better for a coulda-been to remain a never-was. ⚽

1920

DRONGO THE DRONGO

'G'day yer old bastard, beaut arvo.'

'Bloody oath. What are you pricks up to?'

That's fair dinkum how blokes talk beyond the Black Stump – deadset, I'm not havin' a lend. Out there, where it's as dry as a dead dingo's donger, everyday conversations are filled with terms of endearment which could easily be taken for terms of abuse. 'Bugalugs', 'ratbag', 'dropkick', 'dill' – all these words are more or less compliments between cobbers; the noises made by a meeting of mates. And I can't tell you how many times I've been told to 'shut the fuck up' because I'm a 'prick' or some kind of 'pretentious arsehole'. Ah yes, good times, great mates.

But we should point out that there's one word you *don't* want to be called; one word that sounds a lot like an insult because, on close analysis, it actually is. In the *Oxford English Dictionary*, a 'drongo' is defined as being a songbird with a glossy black plumage, a black crest and a long forked tail. But in Australia, it means a moron, a loser, an idiot, a schmuck. I don't just mean the sort of person who is so stupid they can't tie their own shoelaces. I'm talking about the sort of person who doesn't even understand what shoelaces are *for*.

And, if urban myth is to be believed, I am also talking about a horse. It's thought that the word 'drongo' dates back to a racehorse of the early 1920s, who got his name from the glossy black bird. Sired by a Melbourne Cup winner, and related to another one on his mum's side, Drongo had a near-perfect pedigree: you might even say he was equine royalty. He certainly looked like a champion, with that big, broad chest, gleaming coat, and long, springy, muscle-lined legs.

At only two years old, he also ran like one. Drongo came second in the VRC Derby in his first few months on the track, and just missed out on the St Leger Stakes. He had the best jockeys, the best trainers and the best prospects of future success. 'Drongo is sure to be a very hard horse to beat,' wrote a journalist in the know. 'He is improving with every run.'

But that journalist actually *wasn't* in the know. In fact, he knew nothing at all. Drongo clocked up five second-place finishes throughout his 37-race career, together with a few solid thirds. But when it came to winning, it just wasn't to be. If you take out a calculator and carefully add up Drongo's victories, you will eventually arrive at a total of nil.

But did he win a place in the dictionary? It's thought that, after the thoroughbred ran (and lost) his final race, punters began to use his name when they wanted to describe a certain type of horse. A horse who looked good but actually wasn't; a certain winner who was certain to lose. To be 'a Drongo' was to be a failure – or, at least, a horse who hadn't quite fulfilled hopes. And, after a while, the word came to mean 'hopeless'. And to be used to describe humans as well.

But could this just be a big, urban myth? Ladies and gentlemen, boys and girls, let's return our attention to the drongo *bird*. As it happens, they're a bit hopeless too. They're a bird that, when they migrate in winter, frequently fly to a place that's even colder than the one they just left. Could drongos be the original drongo? Call me a drongo, but I think that the answer is 'yes'. ⚽

SPOOKY LEGENDS

'IF THERE'S SOMETHIN' STRANGE IN YOUR NEIGHBOURHOOD, WHO YOU GONNA CALL?' I WOULD SUGGEST THAT YOU CALL NO ONE. (YES, EVEN IF 'IT'S SOMETHIN' WEIRD AN' IT DON'T LOOK GOOD'.) AS THIS SECTION SHOWS, THERE'S SOMETHIN' STRANGE IN PRETTY MUCH *EVERY* NEIGHBOURHOOD, OR AT LEAST EVERY FAIRLY OLD HOUSE.

We've all heard spooky noises and smelt unusual smells. We've seen doors slam shut for no reason and objects that seemed to move by themselves. We've had a sudden feeling of dread when we walked into a building, or a feeling that we're being watched. So, 'somethin' strange' is generally not so strange. And the fact that it happened in an old house does not mean that the house once hosted a murder.

I'm sure that you know all this – the people in this section, however, do not. Here are some all-Australian ghost stories believed by some people who are probably not all there.

1821

· · · · · · · · · · ·

A WISE MAN?

Apart from cowboys, soldiers, founding fathers, and presidents other than George W Bush, there's nothing more important to American mythology than the stupidly rich 'self-made man'. Americans love anyone who was born in a log cabin, and then managed to pull himself up by his bootstraps. It doesn't matter whether his name was Carnegie or Rockefeller or Morgan or Hearst; all that matters is that he had heaps of money, and that he got it by exploiting the poor.

In Australia, we tend to be less keen on these types of people. (Call it the 'tall poppy syndrome'. Or maybe basic decency.) But this seems like a pity when there's such a great example to hand. A sweet little town on the Hawkesbury River, about sixty kilometres north of Sydney, Wisemans Ferry got its name from the self-made man who built and ran its very first ferry.

Former convict Solomon Wiseman also built a popular pub called the Sign of the Packet and a two-storey residence called Cobham Hall. He saw himself as 'king of the Hawkesbury', according to the *Kuringai Examiner*, and was forever strutting about with 'a swallowtail coat, a flowery vest, polished boots and a dress sword. He looked more like a Lord Mayor than an inn keeper.'

But Wiseman was no do-nothing council politician – he was a can-do capitalist, an ideas man with verve and pluck. His particular idea was to only ever employ convict labourers who'd won a provisional 'ticket of leave', and to pay them in scraps, whips and pain. The king's 'harsh treatment' caused many of his subjects to try to swim for their freedom, and those who succeeded were often recaptured and hanged. The vast majority drowned, however, because, well, they were wearing leg-irons.

Other 'ticket-of-leavers' did not try to escape his harsh treatment, but responded by working as hard as they could. It's said that if Wiseman really liked their work, he would provoke a quarrel just before their release. 'The worker would be lashed and his ticket of leave withheld for another year.'

You can see some of these labourers' ghosts, if you ever sail along the Hawkesbury River – but if you see a spectral woman, it's Wiseman's wife. She, he supposedly threw out of a second-storey window, after a 'heated argument' in his pub. 🐈‍⬛

1826

FISHER'S GHOST

People kill each other for all sorts of reasons, from politics and religion, to jealousy and revenge. Loud, repeated playing of that Red Foo song 'Let's Get Ridiculous' could well feature somewhere on the list (or it will soon if my neighbour doesn't stop it).

The most common motive, however, is money. Filthy lucre has prompted plenty of dirty deeds over the years, as Australia's most enduring ghost story attests.

The story of 'Fisher's Ghost' begins in 1816, when a young convict arrived on our shores. Fred Fisher eventually won himself a 'ticket of leave', which enabled him to buy a thirty-acre farm in Campbelltown, right next door to the farm of another 'ticket of leave' man, George Worrall.

The two men were as thick as thieves (so to speak), so no one was particularly surprised when Worrall announced that Fisher had given him his farm, and decided to go back to the Mother Country.

But *why* did Fisher decide to go to the Mother Country? And why did he do it so suddenly, without saying goodbye? People in and around Campbelltown pondered this question for a minute or two. Then they shrugged and got on with their day.

Four months later, however, it's said that a 'respectable local man' named John Farley was doing whatever it is that respectable local men do, when he saw a ghost that looked just like Fred Fisher. Fisher's ghost didn't say anything. But it pointed a finger at a paddock nearby.

At first, Farley's tale was dismissed by the critics (a fate that I'm pretty sure will befall this book). But since Fisher's sudden disappearance was – well, all things considered – kind of odd, a policeman eventually decided to have a look around the paddock. He soon discovered Fisher's body buried next to a creek.

It didn't take the police too long to arrest George Worrall – or too much torture to make him confess. He was hanged by the neck in February 1827, but Fisher's ghost is still seen to this day.

I'll try to keep Worrall's punishment in mind the next time I hear Red Foo ...

1830

THE MERCILESS CAPTAIN LOGAN

There are many reasons not to go camping. They include flies, dust, heat, cold and the deep, pervading sense of hopelessness and despair that tends to kick in after a day without television.

But there's an even better reason not to go camping, should you be planning to pitch a tent near Logans Creek. People who've done that have been known to run, screaming and wailing, from a ghost who looks set to kill. (Though, I myself – if it was day two or three – would probably just stand there and embrace sweet death.)

Not far from what's now Ipswich, Logans Creek is where Captain Patrick Logan of His Majesty's 57th Regiment of Foot met his sudden (and very well-received) death. In charge of the Moreton Bay penal settlement during the 1820s, Logan essentially saw his job description as 'torturing convicts', and it was a job done professionally and well. Described as 'cruel', 'merciless', 'feared' and 'despised', he flogged them before breakfast, and then he flogged them before lunch. The afternoons, he liked to set aside for more floggings, and floggings tended to take up his evenings as well.

Every now and then, however, 'the Fell Tyrant' liked to put down his whip, and have a wander around the local terrain. On one such expedition, he was attacked and killed by a local Aboriginal man – and it's safe to assume that the convicts let out a cheer.

The next day, however, they screamed. Around midday, some of the prisoners were working on the riverbank when they spotted Captain Logan sitting on a horse and waving to them from the far side of the river. The details have been recorded on the very impressively designed Brisbane History website:

> *None had any doubts about who it was. Two of them downed tools and hastily launched the punt that was used to ferry people across the river and rowed over to pick up their Commandant ... (But) when they arrived on the south bank ... there was no sign of Logan. He and his horse had vanished into thin air.*

'At that time Captain Logan's battered body was growing cold in a shallow grave in the bush seventy kilometres inland.'

1830s

UNSAFE HARBOUR

The best medical advice you could get in the olden days was to steer well clear of doctors. It wasn't just that these people weren't especially helpful; it was that they actively made things worse. Feeling a little fluey? Why not try a spot of bloodletting, or some of this exciting new medicine called 'heroin'? Having a little trouble in the genitals region? How about some mercury or arsenic?

But for all the 'soothing syrups' that were made out of opium, and toxic tonics that could cripple or kill, you'd still be better off sipping Dr T Barnum Duffy's Elixir of Life than you would spending a few weeks in quarantine. A device for protecting society from sick people – and making those sick people a great deal sicker – quarantine basically involved waylaying every ship before it arrived in a harbour and forcing anyone who might be ill to get off. All sailors and passengers who might conceivably have a contagious disease would immediately be placed under thick lock and key until they could convince the authorities that they were perfectly well.

But very often, of course, they couldn't ... because they had gone and caught a disease while locked up in quarantine. Basically one big petri dish – a place where bacteria could really let it all rip – the North Head

Quarantine Station in 19th-century Sydney was a great place to get yellow fever, typhus or smallpox, so long as scarlet fever didn't kill you first. Also a fertile source of Spanish influenza and major breeding ground for bubonic plague, this small set of buildings just off Manly Harbour boasted 'truly appalling conditions with a sense of misery, wretchedness and disease present everywhere'. About five hundred people are thought to have died there, and many more lost their will to live.

The Quarantine Station was torn down in 1984. But is it any wonder that its victims still haunt it?

1838

BORN TO DIE

And am I born to die
To lay this body down.
And must my trembling spirit fly
Into a world unknown.
A land of deepest shade
Unpaired by human thought.
The dreary regions of the dead
Where all things are forgot.

So goes the epitaph on an old gravestone in a NSW town called Castlereagh: cheery stuff, as I'm sure you'll agree. The gravestone sits above the body of one Sarah Marshall, a convict who arrived in Australia in 1818 and left for the 'land of deepest shade' twenty years later.

Those two decades were productive, as far as childrearing went: Sarah had no less than eight kids with John Simpson, a former convict who found work as a tailor. But what she *couldn't* produce was a marriage certificate: the two never walked down the aisle. Having kids out of wedlock was enough to make you a 'slut', 'tart' or 'harlot' in those enlightened times, a fact that may have contributed to Sarah's demise.

All we know for certain is that a group of anonymous drunks followed the 42-year-old 'harlot' as she made her way home one dark night, and clearly became annoyed when she 'played hard to get'. Sarah Marshall was brutally raped, beaten and murdered in what was later, and ever-so-sensitively, described as 'a fit of lust'. Her attackers were never found.

You can understand, then, why Sarah's ghost may not be especially friendly to any male who makes his way past her gravestone. 'Paranormal investigators' who are in possession of a penis frequently say that it gives them shivers.

But maybe they're just shivering with embarrassment? Because, well, you know ... they're 'paranormal investigators'.

1840s

TASSIE DEVILS

Ghost-sightings are a lot like certain drugs: once you've had one, you just want more. You tell yourself that you can take it or leave it alone; that it's just a social thing you can give up any time. But before long, you've gone and got addicted, and need an intervention from your family and friends.

Nowhere is this truer than at Port Arthur, Australia's most haunted penal settlement. A place for the hardest and nastiest convicts (i.e. the ones who were already convicts, and then went and did something again), Port Arthur was a living hell during the 1830s and 1840s – a place where, on a good day, you'd only be flogged once or twice, and where solitary confinement was a nice little treat.

Nowadays Port Arthur is not so much a prison as a tourist trap – one with a great many ghosts. 'It's by far the most haunted spot in Australia,' says one of Port Arthur's innumerable 'ghost tour' guides. 'Nothing is fabricated, there are no tricks. It is about real people's stories.'

Real *dull* people's stories. With over two thousand reports of unexplained odours, mysterious footsteps and 'strange emotional reactions to the buildings', you could write a book about all the ghosts at Port Arthur, though I'm not sure if I'd want to read it.

The first ghost to be spotted in the Tasmanian settlement – the gateway ghost, if you will – was supposedly seen at the house of the prison's chaplain, a man called Reverend Hayward:

> *The Hayward family had been visiting Melbourne and the Reverend Hayward had hurried back leaving his family to follow,' wrote George Gruncell way back in 1870. 'One night after his return, the doctor at the settlement, seeing lights from the upstairs rooms of the Parsonage, thought that the parson's wife and children had returned. When he went to welcome them home, he found only the Reverend Hayward and a servant. No one had been upstairs and when the rooms were inspected they were found to be in darkness. But others in the settlement had also seen the lights and assumed that the family had returned.*

Yawn.

1842

· · · · · · · · · · · ·

THE LADY IN BLACK

Nobody likes a back-seat driver (quick shout out to my partner, Jenny). There are the ones who tell you to go slower just because you're breaking the speed limit, and the ones who tell you to change lanes because you're on the wrong side of the road. Incredibly annoying are the ones who yell, 'Stop!' when you're about to hit a car or a tree, and then complain because you smashed up their Holden. (As you may be gathering, I'm not a great driver. My insurance company has been aware of this for some time.)

The worst backseat drivers, however, are the ones who turn into ghosts. Especially ghosts who have spent over a century clinging on to the back of vehicles and causing their drivers to swerve, crash and die.

One such ghost is 'the lady in black', a phantom who was first immortalised in Henry Lawson's 1891 poem 'The Ghost at the Second Bridge'. 'A mournful figure dressed in black', she does her thing along the Victoria Pass, an old road in and around the Blue Mountains.

Beyond that, details are hazy; some people say that the lady's 'eyes shine in the dark like a tiger's' while others insist that she's headless. But all agree that she's the ghost of one Caroline Collits, a girl who came to live in the Blue Mountains in the 1830s and was forced to marry ridiculously young. Eighteen months in, the seventeen-year-old left her husband, William, to live with her younger sister, who happened to have a husband as well. *His* name was John Walsh (aka 'that violent drunk'). And rumour had it that all three shared the same bed.

Whether or not there really was a *ménage à trois* shall remain *un mystère*. But William Collits certainly believed the rumour, and he angrily confronted Caroline and John about it in Victoria Pass.

Being a violent drunk, John Walsh reacted violently and drunkenly. 'Run, run, he has got a stone and will murder you,' Caroline screamed to her husband – and run William intelligently did.

The worst backseat drivers, however, are the ones who turn into ghosts. Especially ghosts who have spent over a century clinging on to the back of vehicles and causing their drivers to swerve, crash and die.

In the event, she should have run too. *The Sydney Herald* reported that Caroline's body had been found on the Pass the next morning, 'face and head covered with blood and bruises, and a frightful wound in the temple'. It had 'evidently been inflicted by a large sharp jagged stone, one corner of which fitted into the wound, and was clotted with blood and hair'.

John Walsh was hanged a couple of years later. And drivers have been crashing at the site of the murder ever since. 🐾

1843

OOPS

There's not much fence-sitting when it comes to capital punishment – you think that either it's right or it's wrong. To my mind, it's a cruel and barbaric practice, and anyone who disagrees should be shot.

The ghost of John Gavin would probably take my side, so if you ever see him haunting Fremantle Arts Centre, be sure to stop and say hello. The oldest building in Western Australia (and probably still the nicest), the Fremantle Arts Centre started life as a jail. Its youngest ever inmate was fifteen-year-old Gavin, a juvenile delinquent who was accused of murdering a farmer's son – and pleaded not guilty all the way to the noose.

Unfortunately, 'it turns out that he probably *was* innocent,' says local tour guide Geoff Morgan. Not only did police find no real evidence ... or opportunity ... or motive, but 'in recent years they've discovered that the farmer's wife, the boy's mother, was suffering badly from postnatal depression'.

But hey, we all make mistakes: no use crying over spilt milk etc. 'He was a lightweight kid, so they ended up tying chains to his legs to give him a bit of weight so he'd break his neck when he went through,' says Morgan. Job done, the hangman then 'just took him down and buried him in a hole, just down here in the sand hills somewhere, unmarked'.

So is it any wonder that his spirit is still with us? Young Gavin is a ghost with a grudge. 'The shipwreck gallery just down here is said to be haunted and that's said to be John Gavin. People hear things bumping around in the shipwrecks gallery. People see stuff out the side of their eyes.'

Of course, we need to be rational about all of this: intellectual precision is everything in these matters; it's very easy to get carried away. The stuff that some people see out the side of their eyes could be something completely different.

She has this thing for redheads, [so] often redheads in or around the arts centre feel their hair being pulled.

E.g. a different ghost. Fremantle Arts Centre is also said to be haunted by a 'madwoman' whose red-headed daughter had been kidnapped. In 1864, you see, the building ceased to be a jail and turned into a home for the mentally ill. 'This lady was placed in the asylum (after) her daughter had been abducted. She obviously couldn't handle the fact her daughter was never found and they had to place her in the asylum.

'She spent all her time there just looking for her [red-headed] daughter and she ended up jumping out the window at the front and killing herself. She has this thing for redheads, [so] often redheads in or around the arts centre feel their hair being pulled.

'This happened to [a girl] on a tour one day … she came up to me white as a ghost saying, "I've just had my hair pulled" and she was a redhead. Her mother came up to me afterwards and said "Look I've got a photo of this, I just happened to take a photo" and she'd got that photo there, with the daughter and I don't know, something blurry behind her.'

Something *blurry*? Eek. I think that there's a ghost in some of my photos too.

1877

. . . . · . . · · . ·

TRUE LOVE AT OYSTER BAY

I'm not all macho when it comes to love stories. (Though if truth be told, I'm not really all that macho when it comes to anything. I try to be, every now and then – like when I'm in a hardware store, say, or a country pub – but it just never quite seems to come off.)

Anyway, my point is this: there's nothing wrong with a man liking a rom-com, or flicking through *Fifty Shades of Grey*. We all have a need for romance and excitement, and that's obviously not something you'll ever get from your spouse. There's something inherently satisfying about a person risking everything for love, so long as that person's not you.

Catherine Spense was one such person. And, by all reports, she's now one such ghost.

Born in Ireland in 1840-something, and so poor she could barely afford a potato, Catherine married her one true love, Cathal, in 1860-something, and the couple moved to England in the hope of earning a crust. Jobs were hard to get, however, so Cathal eventually resorted to *stealing* a crust – and was sent to Australia as a convict in chains.

Still determined to earn that crust (she was probably getting sick of potatoes), Catherine didn't allow Cathal's deportation to get her down. Like a true romantic heroine, she just got up and got herself a job. Our fair lady spent the next ten years working for a wealthy old lawyer, gradually making herself indispensable and never once revealing the hole in her heart. And, as it happened, this lawyer had zero relatives, so when he died, he left his fortune to her.

Conveniently, he chose to die in 1877, the very year Cathal was due for release. So Catherine stuffed all her money in her suitcase and set off to Albany, Western Australia, all the way over on the other side of the world. When she arrived, she was told that Cathal was alive and well, and living in Oyster Harbour, across the bay. She sent a message for him to cross the bay in two days' time, and she would be waiting there, sitting on shore.

Two days later, Catherine was indeed sitting on the shore – and then she stood up when she saw a little boat. Her one true love was in that boat. And when he saw her, he stood up too. He waved. He blew kisses. He shouted sweet nothings.

And then he fell off and drowned.

People say that Catherine 'collapsed and died of a broken heart', and that her ghost haunts Oyster Bay still. But, then again, people say a lot of things. You should hear what they say at my hardware store when they think that I can't hear.

1880s

· · · · · · · · · · ·

HELL HATH NO FURY

1880s Melbourne was a marvellous place to be. Thanks to the Victorian gold rush (and a land bubble that was all set to burst), the little village had become one of the world's biggest cities – and very likely its richest as well. Migrants just kept on flocking to 'Marvellous Melbourne', and a dozen new buildings seemed to appear every week. Everywhere you looked was a shiny turret or a spanking new tower, some kind of spire or a big, golden dome. The town's long, broad streets were filled with glossy shops and well-dressed people, and there was no shortage of restaurants and pubs.

I could go on and on. In fact, I think I will. Melbourne was a modern marvel. It was a city of gas lights and cable trams; of hotels and banks. It had state-of-the-art schools and it had stained-glass churches; it had libraries and galleries galore.

And let's not forget that it also had prostitutes on every street corner, plying their wares. Life, for these women, was not always so marvellous – and one had it even worse than most. Urban legend says that Young & Jackson, the famous pub opposite Flinders Street Station, is still haunted by the ghost of a 'gorgeous young lady' who was murdered in a laneway nearby.

She's said to be a vision splendid who lures sleazy men like a magnet – and then becomes a vision hideous when they're a few feet away. She suddenly grows old and visibly ill, her skin wrinkling and then eventually peeling in thick, white strips from her face.

'Unfortunately, in those times, murdered sex workers would go largely unnoticed and danger was seen as part of the profession,' says local 'ghost tour' guide Ross Daniels. So it's fair to say that she's a ghost with a grudge. With porcelain-white skin and a pink parasol, shell-like ears and a nice little nose, she's said to be a vision splendid who lures sleazy men like a magnet – and then becomes a vision hideous when they're a few feet away. She suddenly grows old and visibly ill, her skin wrinkling and then eventually peeling in thick, white strips from her face.

But there's still, of course, a reasonable chance that the sleazy man remains keen to do business (beer goggles being what they are). So she then pulls down the neck of her dress to reveal a bloody wound on her throat, and lets out a 'hideous scream'.

It does not, all things considered, sound like an ideal sexual experience. But I dare say that we've all had worse. 🐈

1885

THE DARK SIDE OF DUNTROON

A career in the military may well have something going for it, but if so, I missed the meeting. As far as I can tell, it just seems to involve getting up very early so you can get yelled at a lot, and then marching around in an ugly green uniform. And if all *that* goes well, your reward is a visit to a developing country where people who have guns want to kill you.

On top of that, you may have to deal with a ghost. Canberra's oldest building, Duntroon House, is now home to the Royal Military College (a sort of finishing school for senior officers, and other violent types). But, if urban myth is to be believed, it's also home to the ghost of one Sophia Susanna Campbell – a 28-year-old woman who lived there back in 1885 and died by falling from one of its windows.

Was it murder? Manslaughter? Some sort of Inspector Clouseau-style clumsiness? Sophia's medical certificate says that she actually fell due to a cerebral haemorrhage, but since that explanation's a little bit boring, it tends to be overlooked.

All we know for a fact is that sometime during the 1970s, residents of the Royal Military College 'started to report glimpses of a glowing ghost of a young woman in 19th-century period costume [or at least so says the *Sydney Morning Herald*]. Soon after, some residents also complained that a bed, freshly made in the morning, would be found as if it had been slept in later in the day, with pillows hurled around the room.'

As you might have guessed, this first-floor room once belonged to Sophia. 'It has also been reported that, on many occasions, windows mysteriously open in her locked room.' And on *another* occasion, let it be noted, 'a distressed mother complained of seeing a ghost standing in front of her four-month-old child'.

Scary stuff. By all means, join the army if you really want to (as some bumper sticker once put it, it's a great way to visit exotic places, meet interesting people, and then get out a gun and kill them). Just don't say that I didn't warn you ... 🐈

1887

· · · · · · · ·

THREE FOR THE PRICE OF ONE

Australia's oldest shopping arcade is full of old-fashioned bargains. Visitors to this 100-shop hallway in Rundle Street, Adelaide, don't just have a chance to buy some competitively priced Tupperware – they can also see not one, but an astonishing *three* ghosts for free.

The oldest ghost is, of course, Francis Cluney's. He was a caretaker back in 1887 who didn't seem to take great care of himself. The story goes that one night, Francis saw a flickering light in the arcade and clambered up on a stool to investigate. But the stool collapsed, taking the father-of-five down with it, and he fell right under the wheels of an electrical generator. Don't worry, though, the story has a happy ending: the generator proceeded to grind him into grim little bits.

'Friendly Francis' has haunted the hallway ever since, according to innumerable witnesses. One of them is the daughter of Bronwyn Berry, the owner of the arcade's dry cleaner. 'She was in the shop one morning before the arcade opened and heard the EFTPOS machine beeping,' Bronwyn once told a local newspaper. 'She said, "Francis, if this is you, beep again," and the machine began beeping furiously fast.'

'We're quite sure it's him,' says another shopkeeper, Sharon Leaney, of the strange footsteps they sometimes hear. 'He seems friendly, and no one seems spooked by him. We think he's just keeping an eye on things.'

The arcade's 'resident psychic', Joan Lesley, has also been keeping an eye on things – and she's spotted a second ghost: a mother who murdered her child. 'There's a woman here but she won't tell me her name,' says Lesley. 'She smothered her child with a pillow and is too ashamed to identify herself.'

We can, however, identify Adelaide Arcade's *third* ghost as the wife of one Thomas Houghton. He apparently shot her one hundred years ago, right outside the arcade – only she managed to stagger inside before breathing her last.

So there you go: three great ghosts in one convenient CBD location. And they're all yours for just the price of a parking spot.

Though on the down side, you'll still be in Adelaide. 🐈

1888

THE PHANTOM OF THE THEATRE

I've seen some pretty scary stuff at the Princess Theatre in my time (e.g. *Legally Blonde: The Musical*). The 2002 production of *Mamma Mia!* still has me waking up screaming at night, and all I can say about *Dirty Dancing* is, close your eyes and run.

On the upside, however, I never saw *Faust*. From all reports, that could have been even worse. The Melbourne theatre's 1888 production of the iconic German opera (in which a scholar sells his soul to the devil in exchange for all sorts of stuff) featured a famous baritone called Frederick Federici. But he didn't feature for all that long.

The famous evening show saw Signor Federici (whose real name was Fred Baker) perform the role of Satan in his usual style. After crooning away for an hour or six (while male members of the audience coughed, fidgeted and were shushed at by their wives), the Maestro finally arrived at the grand finale. This is the bit where Satan ensnares Faust in his blood-stained claws, sings for a bit and then descends into hell. (The pits of hell, if you've ever been curious, look a lot like the basement underneath the Princess Theatre's main stage.) The scene involved ropes and pulleys, smoke and flames – and a whole lot of shrieks, howls and drums.

The audience all clapped. The singers all bowed. And there were plenty of people who later swore that Frederick Federici took a bow too.

But the star did not, in fact, return to the stage. It turned out that he'd had a heart attack while he was being lowered through the trapdoor – and that he'd died before his feet hit the ground. And there his corpse lay, quite literally in hell, oblivious to all the applause from above. As *The Age* snappily put it, in a page-long report the next day, 'nothing more weird and melancholy than this unlooked-for and highly sensational occurrence has been recorded in connection with the stage'.

So who the hell did his cast members see, then? There was only one logical answer: his ghost. An 'ethereal figure in evening dress' has haunted the theatre ever since. And he's never even paid for a ticket. 🐈

1890s

MURDER IN MIN MIN

Queensland may well be beautiful one day and perfect the next, but what about its many legions of the violent and tortured undead? The tourist board won't ever tell you about all the ghosts there that want to kill you, but here at Affirm Press we are fearless.

Well, okay, perhaps not entirely fearless: the Min Min light does sound a little unnerving. An unusual and more or less unexplained phenomenon that's still often witnessed in western Queensland, the Min Min light is a strange 'moon of light' that can appear out nowhere. Roughly tree-height, it's said to 'dart hither and thither' for a bit, and then abruptly vanish into thin air. Scientists say that it's probably 'bioluminescent fungi' or something multisyllabic like that, but none of them quite know for sure.

Urban legend, however, *does* know for sure: the Min Min light is a series of ghosts. Specifically, it is the ghosts of some seedy types who were murdered in the Min Min Hotel, a violent pub from the distant past. As Bill Beatty wrote in 1947:

No spots on earth were lower than some of these western shanties of the Queensland of seventy-odd years ago ... the Min Min Hotel was regarded as the worst of these vicious dens ... Dispensing adulterated liquor and drugs, the Min Min Hotel derived its profits from the process known as 'lambing down' unwary shearers and station-hands, who arrived there with large cheques and still-larger thirsts. Many of these men remained there. The fierce, doped spirits caused their deaths. Others were killed in wild brawls, or were murdered for their money.

Conveniently, the hotel had its own graveyard out the back. But the bodies may not have stayed buried for long.

Conveniently, the hotel had its own graveyard out the back. But the bodies may not have stayed buried for long. If we disregard forty thousand years of Indigenous history (as non-Indigenous Australians are often wont to do), the Min Min light was first seen in the 1890s, a few weeks after the pub burnt down. It's said that one night, a 'greatly agitated' stockman came rushing into the Boulia police station and told the following tale.

'You won't believe me, but it's true,' he said. 'I swear it's the gospel truth! About ten o'clock this evening I was riding not far from the Min

Min graveyard when all of a sudden I saw a strange glow appear right in the middle of the cemetery. I looked at it amazed. The glow got bigger, till it was about the size of a watermelon. I couldn't believe my eyes as I saw it hovering over the ground. And then I broke into a cold sweat, for it started to come towards me. It was too much for my nerves. I was terror-stricken. I dug the spurs into the horse and headed towards Boulia as fast as I could. But every time I looked back over my shoulder I could see the light following me! It only disappeared when I got to the outskirts of the town.'

Who the hell could hear that and think 'bioluminescent fungi'?

The answer is, not the people of Boulia.

1890s

THE CRAWLEYS OF MONTE CRISTO

The world is filled with unlikeable couples, from Gabi Grecko and Geoffrey Edelsten to Kim Kardashian and Kanye West. (And let's not forget Lara Bingle and whoever she happens to be with at any given time.)

But none of these couples, it seems safe to assume, could ever be worse company than the creepy Crawleys. Now a pair of ghosts who haunt Monte Cristo Homestead, a rural mansion to Sydney's west, Christopher and Elizabeth Crawley were the legally registered owners of said homestead between 1884 and 1933.

A 'strange and cruel couple' who rarely, if ever, left the house, the Crawleys had seven children who survived to old age; they also had a great many servants who didn't. The homestead's history reads like one of those Agatha Christie novels where she clearly can't be bothered spending any more time on character development, and so has everyone killed about halfway through. As the team at 'SOuL Searchers Paranormal Investigators' tell it, the list of 'appalling incidents and horrific deaths' at Monte Cristo Homestead includes a maid falling to her death from the balcony and a stable boy being burnt to death. Another little girl died after being pushed down some stairs, and a housekeeper passed away after giving birth.

Another servant is said to have had an intellectually disabled son ... whom the Crawleys kept on a chain in the outhouse. And you can add a few stories of caretakers shot dead, and one or two 'mutilated cats'.

Sound like a good place to live? It did to Reginald Ryan. He and his wife bought 'Australia's most haunted house' in 1963 – and they said that they were immediately greeted by a 'brilliant fierce light'. A little while later, their nephew came to visit, and he was visited in his turn by a 'young woman dressed in white'. She whispered, 'Don't worry, it will be all right,' and then silently vanished into the night.

'Phantom footsteps, strange apparitions and haunting noises' have been a feature of the Ryans' lives ever since. Along with a stream of high-paying tourists ...

1905

TWO GHOSTS, EIGHTEEN HOLES

I don't really need to see a ghost on a golf course in order to feel a sense of horror and dread. If I happen to have played golf on that course before, you see, it will already form a part of my nightmares – every hole a reminder of short putts missed, or a tee shot that I somehow hit backwards. And if I *don't* happen to have played on that course before, then it's just an opportunity to fail somewhere new. A chance to acquire some fresh wounds, rather than just dwell on the old.

Camden Golf Club, however, sounds even scarier than most – and I'm not just talking about all those tricky bunkers near the second green, and that big lake that's beside the eighteenth. The Studley Park venue, sixty-five kilometres south-west of Sydney, has something even spookier. It has its office in a haunted house.

The grand old manor that is Studley Park House, you see, hasn't always been a grand old pro shop. It was once a school called Camden Grammar – a school whose students included fourteen-year-old Ray Blackstone. On 15 October 1905, it's said that Ray and five of his fellow boarders decided to go

for a swim in a dam. This decision was very much against school rules, and those rules were in place for a very good reason: little Ray managed to get his foot caught as he swam his way to one side, and he never managed to swim his way back. When staff members finally retrieved the boy's lifeless body, they put it in the school's cold, dark cellar, where it sat awaiting burial for a number of days.

If Ray's spirit *did*, in fact, depart his body during this time and start haunting all the rooms above, the good news is that it wasn't alone for too long. Little boys need their buddies. Camden Grammar was quickly sold to Arthur Adolphus Gregory, the millionaire sales manager of Twentieth Century Fox Australia, and converted into a luxury mansion. But no amount of money could save Arthur's little son from appendicitis: thirteen-year-old Noel Gregory passed away in the house in 1939.

But, like Ray, his spirit is said to live on. 🐈

1905

THE LADIES' MAN

As a husband and father, I can't help but feel sorry for men who spend their lives sleeping with lots of different women, because I know that, deep down, they feel lonely inside. As a *person*, however, I quite envy them. It all sounds like it could be rather fun.

Patrick Connolly was one of those men. A successful businessman who owned several sheep stations (together with lots of racehorses and pubs), this Perth resident had a way with women – and a pretty loose definition of the word. Paddy's 'conquests' included a teenage girl: one who then foolishly became pregnant. Even more foolishly, she then sought his hand in marriage (turn-of-the-century society not being too fond of bastards, or indeed the harlots who bore them).

But Paddy neatly dodged that trap (woman, where is thy shame?). He stoutly denied that he'd ever even met the wench, and straightaway showed her the door. You could tell that the girl didn't like this by the way that she then went upstairs, to the second floor of the Kalamunda Hotel, and threw herself over the balcony.

And her ghost has been haunting the place ever since. Over the past hundred years or so, the Kalamunda Hotel's guests have heard strange female voices telling them to 'get out' and seen small items mysteriously move. One or two have even seen a ghostly woman in a high-collared Victorian dress. Which seems a little odd, given the girl was Indigenous.

Anyway, let's not nitpick. Another version of the tale has the girl killing herself in Room 24, 'where guests never stay for very long. Glowing lights have been seen in this room when it is unoccupied and the corridor outside is said to be always chilly, even on the hottest days.'

Paddy himself never seemed too troubled by the ghost: he cheerfully slept around for several more decades and saw his horses win seven Perth Cups. Don't believe that people always get what's coming to them. That's even sillier than believing in ghosts. 🐈

1908

THE SCHOOLGIRL AND THE PRIEST

Whenever you see the word 'priest' in a newspaper headline, there's a good chance it'll be followed by 'scandal'. It is a pleasure, then, to be able to use the word 'exonerate'. (Not now, though, sorry. Wait a few more paragraphs.)

Before then, we must visit Kapunda, a small town in South Australia. Picture a smattering of old buildings, one or two pubs, a little park and a couple of schools. It's a perfectly pleasant place to live, so long as you leave after one or two days.

If you see the local ghost, however, I'm betting that you'll leave a lot quicker. Said to haunt Kapunda Cemetery (alongside the ghost of a one-legged cyclist), she's the disembodied spirit of one Ruby Bland, a young girl who lived in the local reformatory one hundred years ago, under the care of one Father Martin. Predictably enough, it's said that the good priest made young Ruby pregnant, and then made her have an abortion with a bit of bent wire. Not unnaturally, Ruby died from an infection, and so – anxious to avoid scandal – Father Martin closed the reformatory and buried her body in an unmarked grave.

238

All this happened in 1908. Or, rather, all this *would* have happened in 1908 if it had happened at all. While there is some evidence to suggest that the priest 'was harsh on the girls, and mentally unfit to care for children', there is no hard evidence that Ruby Bland was ever in his care. According to records, she was actually educated in an entirely different place, and in training to be a nurse at the time of her death.

And while the real-life Ruby Bland did indeed die the day before the reformatory closed, its closure had been planned for the previous six months. And, um, she died of a kidney infection in the local hospital.

Still, where there's smoke ...

No, there is no fire, says 'paranormal investigator' Allen Tiller: 'There were no suicides, no deaths at the reformatory. Such things would be documented. The location was inspected daily by local police, priests and the public, who bought vegetables from the girls and also had the girls do odd jobs like sewing and cleaning. And this rumour that there were babies out there – the reformatory was set up by the government, not just the church. There were nuns out there. They weren't out there aborting babies.'

Exonerated! Praise the Lord! 🐈

1913

THE BABY-FACE OF EVIL

As a subject for entertaining opening lines, people who rape and murder children are about as useful as Auschwitz. So let's just take an entertaining first line as read and say that Ernest Austin (aka Ernest Johnson) was not a man you would want to hire as a babysitter.

A huge, hulking, baby-faced farmhand, with a police record as long as your arm, Austin spent his childhood in a series of 'care facilities', and looked and sounded like 'a feeble-minded simpleton'. After spending a short stint in jail for attempted rape, he moved to Queensland's Samford Valley at the age of twenty-six to get away from the police and try to make a fresh start. But his arrival signalled the end for an eleven-year-old girl called Ivy Mitchell.

Mitchell went missing on the night of 8 June 1913 – and her 'naked and mutilated' body was found the next day. Austin immediately became a suspect despite the fact no one knew his background – because, well, he was clearly a creep. Suspicion turned to certainty when the police compared the soles of the farmhand's hobnailed boots to the bloody footprints at the scene of the crime.

It seems that more or less everyone who attended the burly killer's short trial came away with a case of the creeps. (The *Brisbane Courier* made much of his 'callous indifference' and the 'silly grin' with which he eventually confessed.) And then it was the turn of his fellow prisoners to have a little shiver crawl up the spine. Austin is said to have died as he'd lived: with a smile that made everyone shudder. 'As the executioner released the trapdoors beneath his feet, the murderer began to laugh, all the way to the very end of the thirteen-foot rope. Even then, he tried to force out one last little chuckle from between his lips. It was said that the laughter was often heard in the early mornings in the cellblocks.'

Brisbane's Boggo Road Gaol was never exactly a *good* place to be, but from that day forth it became even worse. For decades, prison lore has insisted that Austin's ghost stalks the cells at night, harvesting souls on behalf of Satan:

> *Prisoners would see a face appear outside their cell door, and when they looked into his eyes they somehow knew it was Austin and that he had made a deal with Satan to deliver their souls in exchange for his own. Having locked eyes with the prisoner, the ghost of Ernest Austin would then come through the door and try to strangle them, driving some to madness.*

As I said, folks, not a great babysitter ... Maybe try busybeesbabysitting.com.au, or somewhere like that. 🐕

1916

BLOOD ON THE TRACKS

'There are many shortcuts to failure, but there are no shortcuts to true success,' says the 'inspirational' American 'leadership guru' Orrin Woodward, who sounds like a bit of a prat, if you ask me.

But in one respect, I have to agree with the 'life-changing' life coach (though if I ever buy one of his 'bestselling' books, you have permission to slap me, and then steal my wallet and set fire to my house). Shortcuts often lead to failure. And this is particularly true if you take a shortcut through a train tunnel. And, well, get squashed by a train.

In 1916, a woman did just that. It's said that forty-something-year-old Emily Bollard decided to pay a visit to her brother in Picton, a small town in New South Wales. His farm lay on the other side of the Redback Range Tunnel – a 592-foot-long train line that wends its way right through a hill.

But who can be bothered climbing up and down a hill? Or, for that matter, consulting a timetable? Not Emily, that's for sure. We'll never know what she thought when she came face to face with a train in the middle of the tunnel, but she doesn't appear to have been a woman who really thought all that much.

'In the years that followed,' say the team at West Sydney Paranormal Researchers, 'reports were made of a woman acting strangely in the tunnel. It is believed by locals that Emily still walks the tunnel.'

But let's not just take the locals' word for it. Investigation is the West Sydney way. 'At one stage the ambient temperature at the tunnel entrance dropped down to 14.7°c,' reported a member of the organisation after some recent on-site 'research'. 'You could easily feel a breeze come down the tunnel towards us. This is quite a common occurrence at the tunnel. Even though the tunnel was extremely dark and no lights were on, the movement of shadows was still detectable. My initial thought was that my eyes were playing tricks on me in the dark, but other team members would mention seeing these shadows at exactly the same time.

'Could this have been the spirit of Emily Bollard?'

My guess is that the answer is 'no' ...

1924

MARITAL TROUBLE

Being married is like having a live-in best friend. Though we're talking about a live-in best friend who kind of annoys you a lot, and whom you seem to annoy in your turn. You can learn a lot of things about another person when you see them day after day (after day ... after day), and one of the things you learn is that they are quite irritating.

But still, this is no reason to murder them. Or, indeed, submit to murder yourself. The occasional frosty look is about as far as my warfare with my partner ever goes. Though, if she's in a foul mood and behaving really badly, I *have* sometimes been known to go into another room and mutter inaudibly.

Sir John Langdon Bonython, though ... he was not a man to mess with. Or so, at least, urban myth says. An MP in the first federal parliament and a former editor of the *Adelaide Advertiser*, Sir John was one of olden-day Australia's great movers and shakers. With a big top hat and shiny silver monocle, he was a man who spent his mornings kicking heads in the boardroom and his afternoons counting piles of cash.

Legend says that Sir John generally liked to spend the rest of the day shagging his mistress – and that this was a hobby which his wife didn't

like. But it ceased to bother her after 9 February 1924, because on that day she died of a stroke.

Or was she murdered by Sir J? The story goes that Lady Bonython confronted her husband about his affair at Carclew House, their grand Adelaide mansion. Not a man for frosty looks, or even inaudible muttering, Sir John – according to urban legend – 'incapacitated' his wife in a fit of rage and carried her up to the Carclew's high tower. He then threw her out the window. And 'when he got down to the grounds below to his wife, he found she was still alive, so he carried her back up the spire and threw her down again'.

All very sordid – and now it gets very spooky. 'A woman in a purple gown has been seen on the staircase and upper levels of the house,' says one

With a big top hat and shiny silver monocle, he was a man who spent his mornings kicking heads in the boardroom and his afternoons counting piles of cash.

of the internet's many paranormal investigators, 'and often her perfume is smelt ... This and the occurrence of disembodied voices, footsteps and objects moving of their own accord have helped with the growth of the Bonython legend.'

Hell hath no fury like a Lady scorned. 🐈

1927

THE SLAUGHTER AT SLAUGHTER FALLS

For reasons that I've never quite understood, the 1990s American girl group TLC sang a song about waterfalls, and warned us not to chase them. If the video clip's anything to go by, the song's got something to do with drugs and/or AIDS, but where a 'waterfall' comes in beats me. Perhaps it's some sort of simile. (Or possibly an analogy or metaphor.)

Anyway, we digress. Though if you ever *do* decide to go chasin' waterfalls, let the record show that you should avoid the one in Mt Coot-tha Reserve. Named after an obscure town clerk called James C Slaughter, the JC Slaughter Falls are perfectly nice – in a small, not-exactly-the-Niagara kind of way. But on the downside, they're home to a ghost.

On 17 November 1927, a twenty-year-old Queenslander named Cecilia Miller visited the falls with her fiancé, Reginald Vaughan – and some people insist that her spirit's still there. Shot in the head at close range, Cecilia's body was found lying next to the falls, not far from an unconscious Reginald, who had apparently been poisoned and was suffering bad wounds. The police eventually concluded that he was also a bad man. The evidence suggested that he had shot his fiancé (something he'd once threatened to do if she ever sought to leave him), then swallowed a pill and turned the gun on himself.

Their hunt for evidence was probably helped by the fact that Reginald said, 'A cloud came over my mind ... I must have been mad to do it.' But still, full marks: well done boys.

But that was just the beginning of the slaughters at Slaughter Falls, if we believe urban myth. Dodgy websites insist that all manner of murders have since taken place at the site, from a butchered food merchant to a chopped-up couple. Could they all have something to do with the ghost of Cecilia – a girl who is said to run around 'silently screaming', with a steel bullet lodged in her brain?

1930s

DR SICKO

It can be hard to tell if you have a bad doctor, but there are generally one or two tell-tale signs. Are their office plants dead? Does their breath smell like whiskey? Do they frequently look a bit blank or puzzled, and then type your symptoms into netdoctor.com?

These are all good and important questions. But the most important one to ask is this: do they ever tie up their patients, take them into the middle of the woods and then conduct gruesome experiments until they die? If your doctor starts doing this, I suggest that you run away. (Presuming that his or her experiment didn't involve removing your legs.)

Anyway, such seem to have been the work practices of one Dr Michael Schneider, a surgeon who lived in the Adelaide suburb of Stonyfell eighty-odd years ago – and whose victims still haunt it to this very day. It's said that Schneider went a teensy bit crazy after his young wife died in a horrible accident that also killed the couple's daughter. Left alone to brood in Clifton Manor, a ye olde house in forty acres of forest, Schneider clearly decided that he needed a new hobby to help take his mind off things, and turned to his patients for a helping hand.

Legend has it that throughout the 1930s, Schneider's neighbours often reported strange sounds coming from his little log cabin. They were said to include tearful cries and blood-curdling screams, and hammering and sawing and screwing.

What was going on in there? Well, my guess is 'absolutely nothing' given that none of Dr Schneider's patients were ever reported as missing or found buried in the forest with three extra heads. But why should we believe all those boring local historians who say that Schneider was actually 'a lovely man' and that the whole story 'is basically an urban myth'?

Whether or not ghosts actually haunt Stonyfell, the fact is that thrillseekers *do*. Drunk teenagers descend on the suburb every Friday and Saturday night, hoping to catch a glimpse of something supernatural (or, failing that, get drunk and smoke ice). The local council recently voted to close the Michael Perry Reserve between 10pm and 5am each night, after a YouTube video about the 'hauntings' went viral. It's an experiment in crowd control that will probably fail.

1940

. . . .

LOCKHART AIR CRASH

For a city with so few people, Canberra has a surprisingly large number of ghosts. Along with the ones already mentioned in these pages, it boasts the spirit of a small girl who burnt to death near Lake Burley Griffin (she apparently got too near a hot iron while wearing a very flammable dress), while the ghost of former PM Ben Chifley can still be seen at the Hotel Kurrajong, the place he was staying when he died of a heart attack.

But to get true value for money – for the most ghosts, so to speak – you need to go to a little hill just outside Canberra Airport. This is because an RAAF bomber once crashed there, killing all ten people on board.

And not just any old people, mind you. Important (or, at least, self-important) ones. Three cabinet ministers were among the crash victims, along with the Australian Army's chief of staff. All on board were being flown to Melbourne for a World War II-related briefing session, but the plane only managed to flutter for a couple of miles. As the *Melbourne Herald* reported the next day, the Lockhart bomber was seen by watchers at the Canberra Aerodrome and the Air Force station to circle the drome, and then rise and head south. It disappeared behind a low tree-dotted hill. There was an explosion and a sheet of flame, followed by a dense cloud of smoke.

> *The Canberra Fire Brigade and ambulances from Canberra and Queanbeyan, across the border in NSW, as well as several Air Force tenders, arrived soon afterwards and fire extinguishers were played on the blazing wreckage. After about half-an-hour, when the blaze had died down, it was seen that the entire undercarriage, wings and structural supports of the plane had been torn away and were a smouldering mass in which were the charred bodies of those on board.*

Prime Minister Robert Menzies was deeply affected by this smouldering mass, describing it as 'a dreadful calamity' in the House the next day.

But ghost hunters just get excited. They still tell tales of a teenager who supposedly fled the forest screaming, claiming she was being followed by an airman on fire.

1980s

UNEASY RIDER

'In the beginning God created the heaven and the earth. And the earth was without form, and void; and darkness was upon the face of the deep. And the Spirit of God moved upon the face of the waters. And God said, Let there be light.'

So, I'm told, goes the first bit of the Bible (can't say that I've read the thing, personally). Perhaps the next bit explains what exactly is going on with that strange light some people see in Port Stephens? That place seems pretty 'void' to me.

If not, we'll just have to rely on urban myth. It says that the mysterious bright light that occasionally pops up in Lemon Tree Passage is actually the ghost of a motorcyclist. Legend has it that the light will only ever appear if you're travelling 111 kilometres per hour – the exact speed that said cyclist was going when he skidded, crashed and died.

Common sense says that the light is probably something to do with the headlights from other cars. Headlights that suddenly appear and then, just as suddenly, disappear, as you and they weave up, down and around the ragged bends of the road. But this book is no place for common sense. If we just stuck to that, it'd be three pages long.

Another thing that common sense tells us is that it's usually a good idea to avoid Australian films. The news that a ('somewhat dissatisfying') film was being released about the Lemon Tree Passage ghost recently prompted two people who have 'seen the light' to describe their experience to the *Newcastle Herald*.

'I was on the road with [her friend] when I was about nineteen, which was twenty-six years ago, and we were coming home after midnight from Nelson Bay ... when a single light out of nowhere appeared,' said Tanya Locking. 'I didn't really think much of it except that it was very close behind me.

'When I started to comment to my friend about the goose riding behind me the light just disappeared. I thought he was going to ram us. While we were chatting the light reappeared again out of nowhere. My friend turned to see it as well. I told her to climb in the back seat and have a look, but she wouldn't, she was too freaked out.

'I asked her to stick her head out the window to have a good look and when she did she looked at me scared, as she said there wasn't any noise that a motorbike would make and we were going too fast for a pushbike. We started to panic and drove faster but the light stayed behind us for at least a half kilometre.

'We were dead set sober that night and straight. It was weird and scary and I was never so happy to get on Stockton Bridge and get back to the lights of the city.'

2000s

THE ANATOMY OF EVIL

Canberra has plenty of real-life monsters – Cory Bernardi, Christopher Pyne ... Barnaby Joyce scares the bejesus out of me, while just typing the words 'Bronwyn' and 'Bishop' is probably enough to give me nightmares for months.

But for more imaginary monsters, we must look outside the government, and inside a rather grey and rather grim art deco building that's very near ANU. Now home to the National Film and Sound Archive, it once served as Australia's Institute of Anatomy.

'Eh? What's that, then?' I hear you say. Well, the Institute of Anatomy was a place where scientists used to study the human body – and store bits of it from wherever they could. Some old lady's heart, some young girl's lung. One or two leg bones, some old guy's lips. They were all there, somewhere, in a box or on a shelf: even the walls were lined with old human skulls. It's an adventurous form of interior design which I must say I'd like to see on *The Block*.

Nowadays, alas, all the skulls are long gone, but the good news is that there are plenty of ghosts. Spooks and ghouls seen at the National Film and Sound Archive reportedly include 'a poltergeist that hurls the circular metal containers of the old-fashioned film strips, a petri dish-throwing poltergeist in an upstairs darkroom and the ghostly vision of a child [who likes to] look up through a grill in the old cinema'.

And all these ghosts can get a little bit aggro, if we believe the local 'ghost-tour guide' Tim. 'Quite a few people get pinned up against the wall by an unknown force in the basement,' he says. 'If that happened to me, I wouldn't be too happy. They struggle for breath as if someone's gripping them around the throat in a headlock and jamming them up against the wall. So that's probably a malicious ghost as opposed to the mischievous ghosts at Old Parliament House.'

I'm sorry, what was that, Timbo? There's a ghost at Old Parliament House *too*?

But, of course. 'Quite a few security guards over the years have requested transfers because of things going on in there,' says Tim. 'Like they've had walkie-talkies ripped off their belt and thrown to the other side of King's Hall when they've been doing the graveyard shift.

'As to who haunts it, it's a bit of a mystery.'

Sorry Tim, but I'm guessing 'no one'. 🐕

2000s

REVENUE FOR THE ROSEWOOD

In one of those excruciatingly jargon-filled articles that take about ten thousand words to spell out the obvious, the fine business minds at *YFS Magazine* recently 'revealed' a series of 'marketing strategies' for readers who own a restaurant or pub. ('In any business, the key to surviving is a steady stream of revenue,' they write. 'To get that steady stream of revenue, customers have to know about your business. Awareness hinges on your ability to market it properly.' Or, in other words, 'ads are good.')

Thinking caps on? Okay then, let's proceed. Some of the strategies listed in *YFS* include 'utilising social media to engage patrons' and 'using promotional materials to build brand recognition'. They then start to say something about 'surveying customers to canvas high-value areas', but I'm afraid that by that time my attention had wandered.

Anyway, dear reader, my point is this. If you own a pub and need to attract some new patrons, you don't actually need any of that stuff. You just need to go get a ghost.

David Pahlke is lucky enough to have three of them. The owner of Ipswich's Rosewood Hotel tells us that 'Psychics who come here see an elderly woman standing on top of the stairs in an old-style black dress and bun hair. I've got photos of the pub from 1914 and 1922 and she is standing on the front veranda. I'd love to know who she was because she is the dominant spirit here.' Speculation has it that this elderly lady is the ghost of the Rosewood's former proprietor, Mrs Roach.

But that's not all, folks! 'Another spirit' at the pub, says Pahlke, 'is a Negro soldier who was shot dead in the back in the doorway of the front bar in the Second World War when there was a US munitions dump just outside of town. The clairvoyants have told us that when he died he was thinking of his mother back in America. He's at peace and doesn't say a lot, but he's still here.

'The third one is the water ghost. He's got red hair, he's Scottish and they call him Rusty.' In case you're wondering, Rusty is a 'water ghost' because the previous owners of the hotel 'reported mysterious wet beds and water dripping off the ceiling'.

But, don't worry, Rusty isn't there anymore. The Rosewood's beds and ceilings are both warm and dry, and yours to enjoy at an excellent price.

2000s

LARUNDEL MENTAL ASYLUM

Google 'Polaris Bundoora' and you'll discover that it's 'the social heart of Melbourne's inner north' – a 'dynamic' and 'diverse' housing development that combines 'contemporary and heritage designs' in a way that 'shines a new light on connected urban living'.

Go there, however, and you might just see a ghost. Polaris, you see, is being built on the site of an abandoned psychiatric hospital. One that was built on an ancient Aboriginal burial ground. And one that was forced to close its doors in 1998 after a public outcry over the treatment of its patients. Pioneers in the use of lithium (and a one-time home to serial killer Peter Dupas), Larundel Mental Asylum is said to have had 'a fearsome reputation for abuse, violence and suicide amongst inmates and staff'.

Between 1998 and 2012, when the asylum lay abandoned, its doors were all kicked down by all sorts of vandals – who then broke all the windows and wrote on the walls. Floorboards rotted, ceilings collapsed, and bats, cats and rats did about six billion shits. But for all the building's rusty syringes, exposed cables and long-dead possums, its scariest feature was a sweet little

259

girl. She seemed to enjoy playing a music box. Or, rather, her sweet little ghost did.

The story goes that (however many decades ago), a five-year-old girl and her older sister were forcefully captured and placed in Dormitory Two:

> They both had severe schizophrenia and were prone to vicious fits. They would smash their heads against the wall or the floor in unison. The only way of stopping them – short of strapping their straightjackets [sic] to their iron bed frame – was to open up their music box. When they heard it, they would stop thrashing and start spinning gently, as ballerinas.

Sad. Awful. Tragic. And now, of course, it gets worse.

> One morning, they were found lifeless, lying together in a crumpled heap their heads smashed open, and their faces bruised beyond recognition. Since that night, the delicate melody has been heard spiralling through the empty corridors of the asylum in the darkest hours of night.

'I never go alone – there is always at least myself and a mate,' says hairdresser-turned-ghost hunter Kristy Jane Dean, who used to visit the derelict asylum from time to time. The 32-year-old says that she's seen 'shadow figures, unexplained mists and flying orbs, which I believe to be spirits' during her nocturnal excursions. 'I am terrified during our hunts, but at the same time I love it … I would love to prove to all sceptics that without a doubt the paranormal exists.'

I expect that the people at Polaris would rather she didn't. 🐈

2000s

HIT MAN, CAT MAN, FISHERMAN

If you didn't know that Melbourne was 'on the move' and 'the place to be', you obviously haven't spent enough time reading our slogans. Also described as '*Me!*-bourne' (though only by some ad guy who hopefully got shot), Australia's second city has always maintained that it's Australia's *best* city – and quite possibly the best place in the world.

As a loyal Melbournian, I am not going to disagree with this. But I *will* say that we need to work on our ghosts. Apart from the handful already mentioned, all our city really has to offer is George, the ghost of Flinders Street Station – and, as ghosts go, he's a tiny bit *blah*. You might see George if you're somewhere near Platform 10, a place that was a popular fishing spot back in the day. He apparently just stands there, holding a fishing rod, staring at the river and looking a bit dazed and confused. If you walk any closer, he'll disappear into thin air – and sorry, folks, but that's the end of the show.

A little more entertaining, so long as we use the word very loosely, is the Cat Man of Altona Homestead. He's the ghost of Edward Goodson, a homeless man who was found murdered in front of the homestead in or around 1909. No one knows who killed Edward or why – but the answer may have had something to do with his fondness for fish. After catching and killing them, he liked to 'keep them around' on his person. It was a smelly hobby that meant he was always surrounded by cats ... and by and large avoided by people.

Anyway, there's no avoiding Ed now. 'They say that when you sit down on the toilet outside the homestead, people feel like a cat is stroking their feet,' says ghost tour guide Ross Daniels. 'It's the Cat Man.'

He apparently just stands there, holding a fishing rod, staring at the river and looking a bit dazed and confused. If you walk any closer, he'll disappear into thin air.

There's also no avoiding Mark 'Chopper' Read, should you ever be walking past his old cell. The 150-year-old Pentridge Prison in Coburg (a place which now forms part of some snazzy apartments) still contains the ghost of Australia's most gregarious hit man, who lived there back in the 1970s. If he sees you, he may well yell, 'GET THE FUCK OUT!' But don't take this personally. He says that to everyone.

And, well, that's about it for all Melbourne's ghosts, I'm afraid. If you're still in need of a really good scare, I suppose you could always try to track down Jeff Kennett.

FAREWELL

So that's it, folks – journey's end. Two hundred or so legends detailed; two hundred or so legends debunked.

But what's that you say? You want *more*? A sequel? Two sequels? Three.

Well, to be honest, I could do with the money. So if you know a great urban legend that won't get a man sued, please email me at:

info@eamonevans.com.au

... and who knows, you may see it in print. Until then, *au revoir*. Or, as the French say, so long.

AND THANKS

To Ruby Ashby-Orr for coming up with this fine idea for a book, and to Keiran Rogers, who suggested I write it. Also to Karen van Wieringen for the design and illustrations, and to Kate Goldsworthy for the proofreading. And to all the others – you know who you are.